Where We Keep the Light

Where We Keep the Light

STORIES FROM A LIFE OF SERVICE

JOSH SHAPIRO

WITH EMILY JANE FOX

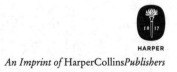

An Imprint of HarperCollins*Publishers*

HarperCollins books may be purchased for educational, business, or sales promotional use. For information, please email the Special Markets Department at SPsales@harpercollins.com.

hc.com

FIRST EDITION

Designed by Bonni Leon-Berman

Library of Congress Cataloging-in-Publication Data has been applied for.

ISBN 978-0-06-346390-5

Printed in the United States of America

25 26 27 28 29 LBC 6 5 4 3 2

For Lori, Sophia, Jonah, Max, and Reuben, with the deepest love and greatest amount of gratitude a man could ever feel. You are my light of all lights.

CONTENTS

CHAPTER I

A Night Guarded by G-d

IT DIDN'T FEEL ALL THAT different, though in thinking about it now, of course everything was. I wish there was a moment I could point to where I could say I saw it coming. Where I sensed something. Where, in my bones, I felt something wasn't right. Or that I'd met the guy before and got a bad feeling, and once we knew what had happened and who had done it, that my brain immediately zeroed in on that interaction and all the pieces fell into place and all of it instantly unfurled before me and made sense. I could wrap my mind around it more if there had been a crescendo or a climax. If I had a clue or an instinct.

None of that happened. In actuality, that whole night, the week leading up to it, felt so perfectly normal that it strikes me even more.

My family had spent that week in early April preparing to host a big group of people to celebrate a Jewish holiday, something we have done dozens of times before. We were ushering in Passover for the third time since I was elected Governor and started holding official events at the Governor's Residence in Harrisburg. The holiday is as many Jewish holidays are—a mixture of solemnity and joy, celebration with a remembrance of suffering. Where once we were slaves, now we were free. Where once we felt pain or separation, now we rejoice together. We tell the story the same way every year. In the same order, actually. Seder, the traditional meal during which the holiday is observed, in fact, means "order," so the predictability of it is the feature. The whole point is that the night should feel familiar.

We had planned to host both nights of Seder with about 150 people over the course of Saturday and Sunday nights—a tradition we started two years earlier. Lori, my wife of twenty-eight years, whom I met in the ninth grade as a teenager at the Jewish day school where we've sent our four kids, insisted. We'd long had our family Seders at her mom's house, where Lori helped prepare.

Passover is particularly important to us now. Since the tragic events of October 7, we feel both a responsibility and pride demonstrating our faith and living it out loud. We know that many feel like it's a trying time to live Jewishly. That doesn't make us shy away from it. In fact, it leads us toward it. We have made it a point to show our faith. In the midst of the protests across the campus of the University of Pennsylvania in the winter of 2023, for instance, Lori and I lit the Hanukkah menorah in the heart of the school's main walk in Penn's Hillel as a way to comfort scared students who were fearful in the face of rising antisemitism on campus and on campuses like theirs across the country. Weeks later, at a Hanukkah party at the Governor's Residence, we lit a menorah from the Tree of Life Synagogue in Pittsburgh, where, in 2018, a mass murderer killed eleven Jews who had simply gathered to pray on Shabbat, our sabbath. It's a community I have stayed in touch with and have become close to in the years since the tragedy. These Seders were an extension of that—a way to show our traditions proudly, from the Governor's Residence, with our family and the community.

Our extended family had been together all week by that

point—my brother Adam, his wife Rena, and their three kids from New Jersey; my sister Rebecca, her husband Jon, and their three kids from California; both sets of our parents. Our daughter, Sophia, recently out of college, had a bunch of school friends visiting. I was busy during the days, but at night I'd come home to the Residence to a packed house, bustling and boisterous and alive. The kids and dogs would run around this gilt-edged Residence or toss a football outside in the backyard. We'd hang around the fireplace in the formal living room. At the beginning, it felt like someone had handed us the keys to a place that couldn't possibly be where we would live, like we were guests in this grand, formal place that wasn't ours. But it grew on us, because we filled it up with us, our four kids and two dogs, our rhythms and jokes and family stories and routines. It quickly became animated by our lives, a home, albeit far more formal. It felt full. Happy, chaotic, us.

That Friday, I took part of the day off and we hauled everyone very early in the morning to the Statue of Liberty and Ellis Island—something, embarrassingly, as good patriotic parents, we'd never done before. As we neared the top of the Statue of Liberty, it snuck up on me, the lump in my throat. The damp April air blew crisp across our faces as we listened to the national park rangers talk to us about our tired, our poor, our huddled masses. Words uttered less these days. Later that morning, as we wandered the halls and took in all the photos lining the walls at Ellis Island, I came across a photo of three young women in 1913 from Kamianets-Podilskyi, the Ukrainian town from which my mom's family emigrated. We called our kids over, showing them their faces and pointing to the halls where their ancestors walked and the tables where they checked in and the doors through which they entered this country.

That night we had Shabbat dinner, as we do every Friday, at our family home before waking up early Saturday to drive to the Residence. Lori needed to get everything organized before the crush of people descended. I had my own stuff to do. I'd led a Seder before, but every year I worry that I don't remember how to do it. It is all laid out in the *Haggadah*—a book for the Passover Seder which explains the story of the Jews Exodus from Egypt—which everyone at the Seder has and goes through together. My brother, Adam, an actual Jewish educator who knows this stuff cold, and I jotted down some notes about all the points I wanted to hit before I saw people arriving outside for dinner. We were still in our sweats, working in my office at the Residence, so I ran upstairs to change before Lori and I greeted everybody.

We met the seventy-five or so guests in the Grand Hall before inviting them into the State Dining Room, where the Seder would begin. Lori and I sat at a long head table with Max and Reuben and their cousins, the rest of our families and guests scattered at round tables across the dining room. Before we began, all of the women were invited to join Lori around a bunch of holiday candles we'd set up near the entrance of the dining room for them to light and say the traditional blessings over to bring in the holiday and begin the Seder.

I started with sharing a few welcoming thoughts. I talked about how privileged we feel to live in the greatest country, where we can all openly celebrate our faiths. That is particularly important in Pennsylvania, founded by William Penn in 1681 as a place where people from all faiths, all walks of life, could come and live and worship freely without fear of persecution.

My brother and I went through the whole Seder, did the requisite prayers, asked some questions, sang the songs. We ate dinner, continued the telling of the Passover story, and by the time we wrapped up, around 10:30 p.m., about forty of us walked back down the Grand Hall to the Erie Room and sat by the fireplace. The kids were running around. Our siblings were cozied up. Sophia and her friends were across the room laughing, all squeezed in together on the big leather couch, surrounded by paintings from Pennsylvania artists. The moment and magnitude washed over me, as it does when I have a catch with one of my kids in the yard outside and someone will walk by and yell, "Hey, Gov!"

Sometimes, in these moments, it's hard to really grasp that I am the Governor, that this is my life. That my children have their holidays and sleepovers here, that the Residence is where their life is unfolding, that it is a home to them.

It was close to midnight by the time I realized that our teenage children and all of the kids were still awake, and to quote a great parenting novel of our time, it was time for them to go the F to sleep. There were twenty of us sleeping over that night, and most of us made our way upstairs to turn in. Reuben, our youngest, came into our room to say good night. I had blessed him earlier during the Seder, so I skipped that part of our usual nightly routine and sent him into his room. Sophia, our oldest, and her friends were still hanging out in the basement, where Lori had banished them after they were making enough noise in her room that they were keeping everyone else awake.

Lori and I collapsed into bed by 12:30. We are night owls. And, unfortunately, also early risers. We turned on an old episode of *Seinfeld*, as we do. My mind raced, as usual—about the Seder, about the work on my plate. I was half asleep by the time I heard loud footsteps and urgent banging on our bedroom door. "Get up!" I heard. "Fire!"

"Governor, we have to get everyone out of here!"

I was awake enough to know the voice and the footsteps and the banging wasn't one of our kids. I knew it was the state police, so I quickly woke Lori up, grabbed a T-shirt from my chair at the foot of the bed and a baseball cap, threw on some shoes, and ran across the long hallway that stretches the length of the house. I banged on the doors of every bedroom along with the trooper.

"We have to go," I told Reuben and his cousin as I opened his door.

"Come on, we need to go—there's a fire."

Our two dogs, Bentley and Bo—a Cavanese and Goldendoodle—were asleep in Reuben's bed, where they always sleep. Lori grabbed them as we made our way down the hall. "We've gotta get out of here," I said. We weren't panicked, but we were purposeful.

Max was already leaving his room by the time I got to him. The trooper had said it was a fire, but I didn't see any flames. I smelled no smoke. It wasn't until we were ushered down a back stairwell that we heard fire alarms at all. Sophia and her friends came up from the basement to find smoke in the hallway. Once we were outside, we counted off several times to make sure everyone was safely out of the house and accounted for. Mist was coming down and the air was too cold for the kids to wait outside without shoes and sweatshirts, so we piled them into Suburbans as fire trucks and Capitol Police with all their requisite wailing started arriving, along with more members of our state police security detail.

Emergency personnel were running into the Residence as we ran out. I walked around toward the front of the house and saw what I thought could be a fire in the dining room, where we had just had our Seder, but it was hard to tell because of how far away I was and the glass and the reflection of the emergency lights. Maybe the candles we'd lit earlier ignited something. Maybe a burner in the kitchen was left on. That's what must have happened, I thought as I walked back toward my family.

We were relatively calm and assumed that once the fire was extinguished, we'd all get back to bed. Everyone could sleep in; we had no plans except our second Seder at night. It would be a story that would become part of our Shapiro Seder lore. I could picture all of us around that same fireplace next year, laughing about how tired we looked racing out of the house in the middle of the night in a strange amalgamation of pajamas.

And then I saw smoke starting to billow. Well, I thought to myself, I guess we are not, in fact, going back in to sleep there tonight. The head of our security detail planned to take us to the Capitol and wait things out. It was nearing 2 o'clock in the morning, and I figured we might as well take Sophia and her friends, who were set to return to Pittsburgh the next day, to a nearby hotel, and the rest of us would drive back to Abington to our family home a few miles outside of Philadelphia, to try to get a wink of sleep in our own beds.

We were still under the impression that this was just an accidental fire, an inconvenience, and it would all be fine and settled after a good night of sleep. The important thing is that we were all safe and the brave first responders were doing their jobs. As everyone got situated for the middle-of-the-night drive, the chief of the Harrisburg Bureau of Fire came over to me.

"Gov," he said, meeting my eye. "I want to show you what happened."

As we walked down the hallway into the Grand Hall, where we had all been lingering a couple of hours earlier, I tasted the smoke in my mouth. The bitterness caught in my nose. It was hard to see more than a couple feet in front of me. Some windows had been knocked out. My feet sloshed through the water puddling on the floor. It looked like a bomb went off here, I thought. It still hadn't crossed my mind that it actually had.

Artwork from the New Deal era that had hung on display had literally melted into the walls. Plates we had eaten our Seder dinner on were broken and covered in soot.

The *Haggadah* and my notes were burned so badly only a few short lines of text were recognizable. Everything was charred.

As I looked around at the destruction before me, I couldn't help but think of how everything was a few hours earlier, as we recounted the story of our ancestors escaping bondage thousands of years ago.

Out of the corner of my eye, I saw the wooden table that held all of the candles Lori and others had blessed hours before. It was wet and a little charred, but it was intact and still standing. Okay, I thought, if it had been a candle that had ignited this place like we had speculated, that table would've burned clear to the ground.

I walked over to the chief and asked what he thought had happened.

"You'll be briefed on that in a few minutes," he said somewhat tersely. No further explanation.

Message received. So maybe it wasn't an accident, I realized. I thanked him and the firefighters and made my way back down the hall to rejoin my family.

Now, at that moment, there were a million things racing through my head. Nearly all of them were practical and involved making sure that my family was OK. But there were two greater things I couldn't shake.

For some reason, it came into my head that Haggadot are written in present tense, so that everyone participating and observing the order and retelling the story of our ancestors is doing so as if they themselves are being exiled from Egypt, that these events feel like present-day realities rather than long-ago historical events. Their suffering is our suffering; their freedom, ours, too.

And I remembered that the Torah twice refers to the night of Seder as "a night that is guarded by G-d." *Leil shimurim.* (In Judaism, we do not spell out the whole word of the Creator, instead replacing the "o" with a dash.) It was a night G-d guarded for the purpose of leading the Israelites out of Egypt and one that remains guarded for generations to come. It's so guarded that some rabbis have long said you don't even need to lock your doors. This is why we don't recite the whole *Shema*, a central prayer in Judaism, as part of the Seder and only read the first paragraph instead; a prayer offering G-d's protection is unnecessary on this particular night.

Harm did try to find its way in, but this night had, in fact, been guarded.

*   *   *

As we stopped at the hotel, which was about five minutes away, to make sure Sophia and her friends from Pittsburgh got into their rooms safely, Lieutenant Colonel George Bivens, the second in command of the state police, greeted us there.

"Governor, this was a deliberate act. It was not an accident," he told me, assuring me that the state police were on top of investigating it.

"I want to make sure you and your family are safe," he said

as we walked toward the truck. I was riding home with our sixteen-year-old son, Max. I told the team to keep me updated in real time. I have been through enough active investigations to know that, in the "fog of war"—these early moments—the initial information is not always right. You can't overreact. You can't rush to judgment. You have to be calm, patient, steady. It was the middle of the night. My kid was exhausted. I didn't want him to know what little I understood, because it could morph before we actually got clarity on what happened. I said to text me instead of calling, so I could keep this quiet as we drove the hour and forty minutes to our family home in Abington, just outside of Philadelphia.

I had a knot in my stomach. I was desperate to talk this all through with Lori, to steady myself with her. I needed to process what had just happened and how it had happened, to review the timeline of that night and come up with a plan. How would we talk to the kids? What was there even to say?

Who would want to do this?

Was this because we are Jewish? Because I'm a Democrat? Did I take a position on some issue that caused this person or people to bring such violence into our home?

Was this my fault for putting our family in the spotlight?

I kept cycling through all the things anyone would want to talk to their wife about in a moment like this. But she was in the other truck with one of our other sons, Reuben, some cousins, and our two dogs. I barely took my eyes off the phone as I watched the steady stream of texts roll in. Someone tried to hurt us. They tried to hurt me, and they tried to hurt my family. We were in real danger. The people who worked in the Residence had been in danger. I wondered who could do this, why they would do this. Was this person still out there? Were they coming to our family home next? How long would it take to figure this all out, to find this person, to get them into custody?

I didn't want Max to pick up on my fear. I needed to look calm.

We got back home at 5 in the morning, and the kids slipped off to bed. In our first moment alone together, I pulled Lori close and told her what I knew. That it was a deliberate act of arson, that we would get a lot more information over the next few hours. She had all the same questions I had. I suggested that we should try to get a little sleep before what I knew would be a lot of craziness to come as the news would become public in the light of day.

I drifted into an uneasy sleep for about an hour. By the time I opened my eyes, my phone was full of more messages from the state police and my team. Dana Fritz, my longtime chief of staff and right hand, had sent me a statement to put out, on which I made one small correction and added how grateful we were to the first responders and police. Nothing could go out, though, until we told all of our kids that it was a deliberate act. They needed to hear it from us. We wanted to be honest, about both what we knew and what we didn't. We don't really make a habit of holding back with our kids, because we have faith in their resiliency. We know that they can handle hard things, and it's important to us that they knew we know that about them. But when the truth is going to be talked about as headline news in the hours and days to come, the first words had better come from us. We needed to be the ones to answer their questions.

We called Sophia, who was still in Harrisburg staying with her friends in the hotel, and Jonah, the only one of our kids who hadn't been there the night before since he was finishing his semester at college. As soon as we told him what happened, he hopped into his car to come home. Sophia would join us later that afternoon, too.

We soon heard the boys rustling in their bedrooms and told them what we knew. Max asked what the house looked like. I showed him some photos and a video that I had snapped with my phone hours earlier. Reuben asked how the police and firefighters knew it wasn't an accident. They know because that's what they do, I assured him.

Then he asked if someone tried to kill us because we are Jewish.

We didn't know, we told them honestly. But we assured them again how protected we were, that we have faith in the state police to keep us safe and catch whoever did this, and how we would answer any questions they had.

I told them I had to return to the Residence, but that I would be back in time for the second night of Seder.

It wasn't going to be a big community dinner in the State Dining Room like we had planned. But there was no question we would be doing one.

*   *   *

I got on the road heading back to the Residence. I had to see the damage in the light of day. I wanted to be close to the investigation to get updates. I wanted to be with my team. I wanted the public to see what I had seen the night before. More than anything, I wanted to show that I wasn't scared. I wasn't going to be deterred. I would show up, get back to work, and do my job.

My team was already on the ground taking photos and video of the wreckage. We didn't want conspiracy theorists questioning whether this really happened. That's the state of the world we live in. What happened happened, and I wanted everyone to be able to see the reality. I asked my team to bring members of the press inside the grounds so they could witness the scene firsthand.

Once our statement and photos went out, I started hearing from just about everyone. Former Presidents Biden, Obama, and Clinton called, as did some foreign leaders from around the world. Business leaders and thought leaders, singers, athletes, my old friends from my school days, newer friends from my kids' schools. The outpouring was immediate and fierce.

It took President Trump a week to call. When he did, from his personal cell number, I initially didn't answer because I didn't recognize the number. I wasn't exactly waiting by the phone for it, and I wasn't looking to do much talking. It was relatively early on a weekend morning. I was up, but the house was otherwise asleep. It had been such a grueling week, the anxieties and uncertainties of it all fraying every nerve ending and sucking up all the oxygen. The phone calls and demands on my time were nonstop. I wanted a little quiet, and this was going to be the day. For a catch with the kids, a walk with Lori. Some semblance of normalcy. I was drinking coffee and reading the news on my iPad when I eventually went to get my phone to see that someone had left a voicemail about fifteen minutes earlier.

The voice was unmistakable.

"Hey, Josh, it's Donald Trump," he said. "I just want to make sure that you and your family are being treated perfectly. We've told our people right at the start that they figure out a hundred percent what this was. Just a terrible situation. But feel free to call me anytime. I want to make sure everything is perfect. I know my people have been doing a good job. They've been working very closely with yours. I authorized it about ten minutes after that horrible event. Can't let that stuff happen. So feel free to call at any time."

Just then, Max walked in the kitchen, sleep still in his eyes. "Was that . . . President Trump?" he asked. I'd imagine he thought he was maybe still in a dream, to hear that coming through my speakerphone. Frankly, it seemed pretty unreal to me, too.

"Yeah," I said. "I should call him back." It would have been rude not to. He's the President. And while no one could accuse me of being a fan, he didn't have to reach out. He didn't have to call. He certainly didn't have to give me his number and tell me to call back.

So I dialed the number he left me, not expecting to get through.

He answered right away.

He asked how my family was holding up. He told me that he was doing everything he could to get to the bottom of it. Max heard it all, a little slack-jawed.

I asked how he was doing, which launched him into a monologue. Gas prices were at two dollars a gallon. The economy was on a tear. The tariffs he had implemented a few weeks earlier—the tariffs that sent the stock market into a nosedive—were already working. He was doing so well, he said.

I raised some important issues for Pennsylvania, including how we needed to protect thousands of steelworker jobs in the Pittsburgh area. He then went through the roster of potential leaders of the Democratic Party and their chances in the next presidential election. He said he liked the way I talked to people and approached problems. He told me he'd be more than happy to work together and form a relationship, and that now that I had his number, I should feel free to call him anytime I needed something or wanted to talk, and that he would take my call. He cautioned that I shouldn't want to be President, given how dangerous it had become to hold the office now.

*   *   *

When I got back to the Governor's Residence that next morning, the state police walked me around the property to show me the suspect's movements, and then they took me to our Charter Room, an ornate conference room with a copy of the Pennsylvania Charter from 1681 on the conference table. They had set up the room as a command center with the state police, leaders from the local district attorney's office, and members of the FBI. We started looking through the surveillance footage from cameras all around the property. There was the guy hopping the fence and hiding in the grounds outside, before smashing a window and climbing inside. We reviewed images of the guy once he was inside the house, knowing that as he walked around in the room right below ours, we were all asleep just upstairs and that there were kids in the basement just below.

Now, I have sat in rooms exactly like this, in this house and in many others, at the head of the table, with law enforcement officers at attention. That responsibility is not new, and I have the confidence and experience to handle what comes next. I know how to take in the hard stuff and make the decision and execute it. I am not always right, but I know how to make the call. And I have the patience to wait out the things that take time despite demands for answers.

But of course this was different. I was the person in charge and I was the victim. I was the leader and needed to be led. I sat there, listening to the facts and watching the footage before me of my life, our home, of what had happened to me and my family.

We would learn later that day that the suspect, Cody Balmer, had turned himself in. Clearly, Balmer appeared to be a troubled individual. Two years earlier, he was charged with three counts of assault for allegedly hitting his wife and ten-year-old stepson. The night before, he had filled beer bottles with gasoline from a lawnmower before walking about an hour to reach the Residence. Once he arrived, he scaled a fence, lay in wait, smashed a window in the reception room with a hammer, and threw one of his Molotov cocktails inside. He then smashed another window in the State Dining Room, where we'd held our Seder, climbed inside, and tried to break through the doors that led to where we were sleeping. When he couldn't, he returned to the State Dining Room frenetically running around before tossing another Molotov cocktail and running out through a double door into the cover of night while the blaze enveloped the Residence. He later told police that he harbored hatred for me. If he had found me, he told them under questioning, he would have beaten me with the hammer. He added that he would not take part in my "plans" for whatever I "[wanted] to do to the Palestinian people." Now, I never have had any "plans," nor do I know what he meant by what I want "to do to the Palestinian people," but the statement seemed pointed. (In October, six months after the attack, Balmer pleaded guilty to attempted murder, aggravated arson, 22 counts of arson, burglary, and other related offenses. Under the plea deal, he was sentenced to 25 to 50 years in state prison.)

"This fire was meant to get that satisfaction of 'I was able to displace the Governor. I was able to attack [him],'" Harrisburg Bureau of Fire Chief Brian Enterline told reporters gathered at a lunchtime press conference. "The Residence has no fire suppression system," he said, and the fire could have easily spread if not for the fact that a large door between the dining room and the hallway leading upstairs had been closed. "It would have been a totally different fire and a totally different outcome, most likely."

This was not the first time I became aware of the fact that people wanted me dead. I am a public figure, in politics, in our modern political climate. I have hardly been shy about my beliefs and my faith, all of which have put a target on my back over the last half decade. That target grew in my time as Attorney General, as I took on the first Trump administration when I believed they had violated the law. The vitriol only intensified after the October 7 attacks on Israel, as I continued to live my Judaism out loud, and it ballooned even further over the course of the summer of 2024, when President Biden stepped out of the race and Vice President Kamala Harris mounted her campaign, and I went through the vetting process to be considered as her running mate.

Still, until that moment, I felt safe. My detail and security protocol were robust. They're trained, strong, and armed. I was never alone. I knew that they would protect me if something went down. I didn't want to live in fear, and I felt like whatever had been out there, I was in a bubble.

But the bubble burst that morning in the Charter Room. People did want to kill me. They were hoping to, and willing to try. They were willing to try to kill my family, too. My wife. Our kids. My siblings and their kids. On a holiday during which we shared our faith and celebrated our freedom. I didn't want to live in fear, and we wouldn't. But my illusion of security and safety was broken. I didn't want to believe in the darkness. That's just not who we are. And, in truth, the outpouring of support buoyed us immediately. As did our gratitude for those who jumped in to protect and care for us and our desire to show our kids how resilient our family and our community and our country are.

I thought about all those candles we had lit at the Seder, the ones we'd initially thought caused the fire alarms to go off and our team to wake us up from our slumbers. I thought about the flames we later saw. The footage I later watched of the arsonist throwing Molotov cocktails into our home, setting the room ablaze. That all of this destruction and fear was overshadowed by the light from the love, support and rallying that came in the wake of it.

Light is the central, definitive metaphor in my faith. It is so present as a symbol that it's mentioned nearly four dozen times in the Torah. Light is genesis, the creation of the world. In fact, the first words of creation are "let there be light." The first time Moses feels G-d's wisdom is through a burning bush. Hanukkah—the festival of lights—is centered around the miracle of a flame lasting for eight days so that Jews could re-dedicate the Temple. Every holiday and Shabbat begins with lighting candles, to signify the beginning of something sacred. When someone dies, candles are lit. In a traditional wedding, a bride and a groom are led to the chuppah—a Jewish wedding canopy—by candlelight. All synagogues hang an eternal flame over the ark where a Torah is kept. Lighting a candle is considered to be a mitzvah, or a good deed, as flames are thought to be connected to the soul—which is why, traditionally, we don't blow them out.

With the realities of what had happened and what it meant for the state of the American political climate, it could have been so easy to descend into darkness. That tensions are so high, divides so great, norms so shattered, and communities so disconnected, that this is how we act. But this wasn't how we'd look at this. We don't look toward the darkness. I knew that we would find meaning from the fire. I knew that we would lean on our faith and our community even more as our way through. I knew that after everything, that's where we keep the light.

*   *   *

I started out the press conference steps away from the burned-out State Dining Room thanking the local, state, and federal law enforcement who were keeping us safe.

"Lori and I—" My voice cracked, and I couldn't swallow the lump in my throat. The tears were coming. Maybe it didn't matter if they did.

I told the reporters that we were overwhelmed by the prayers and messages of support we'd received from all across Pennsylvania and the United States. "Your prayers lift us up," I said. I told them that this attack was targeted. We don't know the person's specific motives yet, but we do know a few truths.

First, this type of violence is not okay. It is becoming far too common in our society, and I don't give a damn if it's coming from one particular side or the other, directed at one particular party or another. It is not okay. It has to stop. We have to be better than this. We have a responsibility to all be better.

Second, if this individual was trying to deter me from doing my job as your Governor, rest assured I will find a way to work even harder than I was just yesterday for the good people of Pennsylvania.

Here's a third truth: If someone was trying to terrorize my family, our friends, the Jewish community that joined us for a Passover Seder in that room last night, hear me on this—we celebrated our faith last night proudly, and in a few hours, we will celebrate our second Seder of Passover again, proudly. No one will deter me or my family or any Pennsylvanian from celebrating their faith openly and proudly.

I hugged my staff, who felt the pain of the moment and who are like family to me, and walked around a bit more. Then I got into my car and drove back to Abington to do just that. Lori, Rebecca, and Rena had cooked all afternoon. Jon dragged chairs into the dining room, where we all gathered around a table to light the candles, to say the blessings, to tell the story of our ancestors who had broken free from selfishness and ego and darkness, toward unity and freedom and light. Before we began we said Birkat Hagomel, which is a prayer expressing gratitude for surviving a dangerous situation.

My brother Adam did a beautiful job leading the second Seder. I sat with Lori toward the back of the dining room on folding chairs. We held hands and tried to will the whirling world around us to just steady a bit. This was family time. This is where we found the comfort and the calm. We told the Passover story in the present tense, as we'd done the night before.

*   *   *

As we settled in to do the Seder at my sister's, our children were adamant about doing something nice for those firefighters who ran into the building as we were being ushered out. One of our kids had the idea to cook for them. Outside of spaghetti—my "delicious dish," as my kids jokingly refer to it—and scrambled eggs, I'm not the world's best cook. But I knew we could figure this out.

Out of the more than a thousand texts from friends and loved ones and colleagues offering help and asking what they could do, Chef Robert Irvine was someone who graciously offered his support. So I took him up on his generous offer, and as soon as I told him what we were thinking, he immediately jumped in to help show our firefighters our appreciation.

On Thursday afternoon, four days after the arson attack, Chef Irvine brought the nourishment to Harrisburg Fire Bureau Station 1, and my extended family and I brought the thanks. We served lunch to all the different fire companies that responded that night and spoke to each one of those firefighters. Toward the end of the meal, I saw John Wardle, the President of Penn Township Volunteer Fire Department, approaching with his father, John Wardle Sr. He was their chaplain, and the elder Wardle handed me a beautiful type-written letter, signed by each member of that volunteer fire department, saying that a few nights earlier at their regular fire company meeting they made a motion to raise five hundred dollars among them to send our family a "love offering, to show our love and concerns for your recent traumatic events. We stand with you to condemn the evil acts thrust upon you all."

It wasn't a "political gesture," he wrote, because he was sure that the department had both Democrats and Republicans. "Please take the kids to a movie or go out to a ball game or whatever you enjoy for a fun family time. We will continue to pray for your family." Of course, we couldn't accept their money, so we put it toward supporting the reconstruction of the Residence. But their kindness and generosity we kept.

He then handed me a paper with a handwritten prayer scrawled across it from Numbers 6:24–26:

The Lord bless you
and keep you;
the Lord make his face shine on you
and be gracious to you;
the Lord turn his face toward you
and give you peace.

I called for Lori and choked up with tears in front of this man. We don't share the same faith. We're not from the same generation. We are registered for different parties, and probably didn't vote for the same folks on the last ballot, but that prayer he wrote for us also happens to be the one that I recite nightly over our children in Hebrew:

יברכך יהוה וישמרך
יאר יהוה פניו אליך ויחנך
ישא יהוה פניו אליך וישם לך שלום

I can't quite remember a time when I was so moved. It was not just the extraordinary coincidence that a prayer that means so much to me and our children was the one that this chaplain handwrote and handed to me. It was also because of something I have learned over and over again in my public and private life: to be open to people of all different faiths and backgrounds to fill your cup, to fill you up and to understand our shared and common humanity. Despite our differences, at our cores, our values are the same. Our humanity is shared. And it's always there, if we choose to see it.

*   *   *

"Hear, O Israel, our G-d, the Lord is one." This is the translation of the Shema, that central prayer of my faith, a declaration to G-d that Jews recite twice a day. Sometimes more, if you're me. I recite it to myself in my quiet moments, as I am waiting on a tarmac to take off, or on a long drive. I use it as a way to call attention to G-d, then to add a more personal prayer. For safety, for good health. For peace for me and others. I say it when I walk our dogs on the trail by the Residence or when the weight of my days bears down. When I am seeking clarity, which is often. Which was certainly that morning, two weeks after we were attacked in our home. In that stillness, I say it in Hebrew. But not this morning. This morning, it was in English, and I was just listening.

"We're grateful, G-d, that last night was not our last night, and we're thankful, G-d, that you've given us another day to do good in the world," Pastor Marshall Mitchell told his rapt congregation inside Salem Baptist Church. Salem has long been at the center of African American life in the Montgomery County suburbs just outside of Philadelphia, though undeniably it is more so since Pastor Mitchell took over more than a decade ago. Salem moved to this chapel about five years ago. For all my years growing up less than five minutes down the road, this was a Catholic church. We played basketball on the hoops that lined the parking lot and football on the lawn outside. Everybody did. In those days, the church was bustling. Years later, I knew Pastor Mitchell was looking for more space, so I connected him with the right people to help him get the space.

The air was chilly, even a week past Easter, but the sun spilled through the stained glass to the head of the altar. "It's good to be in the land of the living this morning—caught on the tightrope between winter and spring, on this chilly morning," Pastor Mitchell said. It is.

"But it's warm in here." It was. And I needed that warmth that morning. My schedule was starting to get back to its normally abnormal hum. Crews were hard at work 24/7 rebuilding the Residence and making security improvements. Lori and I were making sure we answered our kids' questions, of which there were many. We filled their schedules with baseball and lacrosse games and time with their cousins and friends, time with us. We were more purposeful about having dinner together.

Friends and family and colleagues continued to check in. When Lori and I took our daily walks, neighbors stopped us seemingly every block to see how we were doing. It was at once grounding and a reminder of something I wanted to push out of my head. My center was off. When Pastor Mitchell invited me to his church, I knew I would appreciate the warmth from the community.

So here I was, in this Baptist church on a Sunday morning, finding comfort, seeking meaning.

*   *   *

I am often asked where I seek my spiritual wisdom, whom I call on for guidance, on whom I lean to strengthen my connection to my center, to G-d. It is a question that I think comes more often to me than to my colleagues, both because I have been so open about my faith, and because my faith happens to be Judaism. In today's world, that fact calls attention to itself.

I tend to give two answers. The first is Lori. To enter into our home is to understand our faith, as she puts it. It's woven into the fabric of our family, sewn into daily rituals, threaded into how we talk and what we prioritize, knitting us together as our jobs get bigger and our kids grow into their own.

And the second person I often mention is Pastor Mitchell.

Pastor Charles Quann, the longtime leader of Bethlehem Baptist Church about seven miles away, introduced us more than a decade ago. Pastor Quann was the patriarch. To this day, he calls me weekly and leaves a prayer on my voicemail. At the time, I was serving as Montgomery County commissioner, the first Democrat to win that seat in a century and a half. Pastor Mitchell had taken over Salem while he was flying to Los Angeles every week to also work as a Hollywood consultant on movies like *The Life of Pi* and *The Princess and the Frog*.

Not exactly conventional.

Pastor Quann, who is eighty-five, called us each separately. "There's a guy that you need to meet," he told me. "He's the Baptist version of you." He said the same to Pastor Mitchell. "Whenever I talk to him, I feel like I'm talking to you," he said. "Whenever I talk to you, I feel like I'm talking to him. I need to get out of the way and just let the two of you know each other."

And so we did. The way we talk about and wrestle with faith feels easeful. When I hear how he thinks about serving his church, it echoes how I think about serving the people of Pennsylvania. When we talk about why we do this, the root is in the same place. The prayers are not even that different. He caught some looks when he was in a meeting with a group of local ministers a few years ago as they went around the room to talk about who their spiritual influences are. He told them that he talks to me every week.

"About politics?" they said.

No, he told them. About our religion and faith and spirituality. He believes what we believe, he said.

I went to Jewish day school through twelfth grade. I went to synagogue every weekend until at least then. We had multiple rabbis officiate our wedding because there are so many Jewish leaders close to our families, all of whom played a strong role in shaping our lives. We celebrate Shabbat every Friday night as a family. We keep Kosher. Our kids go to Jewish day school.

But I had never been one to live out my Judaism as a history lesson. For me, it has always been about the action of being Jewish, less about the story and the text than about the lesson and the deed—how I take the stories from the Bible and really live out what they're teaching.

What I learned from my years in school and from the way I grew up practicing, and why we chose to send our kids to the same religious school, is the soul work. Above everything else, we learned the work of citizenship, to think critically, to disagree respectfully, to put the needs of others before our own. For me it is spirituality more than religiousness.

Over the last decade, Pastor Mitchell and I have grown closer. We have a Bible study going on a text thread. I'll hear a sermon he gives on a Sunday morning, or I'll call him about an issue I am dealing with that he knows literally nothing about or is far afield from what he is handling in his day-to-day life, and he will point me to a line in the Bible or a story that I vaguely remember from high school but the moral of which I had never really grasped.

Together, we will wrestle with it—a Black Baptist with a Jewish grandfather and a Jewish Governor working through a problem of the day by texting each other back and forth about a line from the Book of John or a passage from the Book of Joshua. This was the way Pastor Mitchell and I worked.

*   *   *

We'd gone rounds like this in the run-up to my election as Governor. The Democratic primary was uncontested, but I knew I could use that period to travel around the Commonwealth, to listen and really learn. This meant that over the course of months in 2022, I would be on the road most days each week, at back-to-back events, crisscrossing the state. I was usually giving some version of the same speech over and over and over. It was a good speech, an important one, hitting all the notes I so believed in—about schools, safety, and economic opportunity. It laid out the foundations on which my campaign was built, and time after time it seemed to resonate. As much as all of this felt like it was working, even still, it was a grind, on me and on our family, being away as much as I was, with little downtime and chance to unwind together.

As the primary neared, I got home late on a Sunday evening. By the time we got the kids off to school the next morning, I checked my watch: I had ninety minutes before I had to get going again. Not exactly leisurely or luxuriating, sure, but it was ninety minutes! Of quiet! Of time, alone, with Lori! Who I'd barely so much as had a few uninterrupted, solo, in-person words with during the last few weeks. Imagine all of the words we could say in ninety whole minutes! We could even talk about the kids. We could talk about what tasks she needed me to get done around the house. Our deal before each election is that she'd support my run but only if I cleaned out the attic first. It would usually be a few days from announcement when I would do a half-hearted job of cleaning up. She let me off the hook for two decades, and it showed when you'd go up there. But at this point, I think Lori mostly gave up on that. I'd take the needling, as long as we could talk about anything other than the campaign or politics. That was really my only wish.

I made us both coffee. I pulled up that day's paper on my iPad, which I'd now get to read, in sweats, at my own kitchen table, next to Lori.

"I am sick and tired of this," Lori said, looking at her iPad, coffee in hand. I know I swallowed hard. Not too hard, I hoped. I thought if I didn't react and stayed still, whatever was coming might just pass. "These Republicans love to claim that they're for freedom and patriotism, but they are full of shit. Telling women what they can do with their bodies, what medicines they're allowed to take, getting in between them and their doctors? Telling kids what books they can read? That's not freedom."

The thing about being with someone you literally grew up with is that you know their rhythms by instinct. You have a fairly good sense of what is around the curves and how to navigate them. I knew well enough that desperate as I was to talk about anything other than the hypocrisy of these Republicans and their faux patriotism—a topic that I know I could rail about for ninety minutes, if not much longer, because it is exactly what I had been doing on the road for months—there was no stopping her.

So I instead snuck a piece of paper, found a random pencil the kids had been using for their homework, and started jotting down what she was saying. I kind of hoped she wouldn't notice that I was taking notes so as not to encourage more talk of politics, but I knew what she was saying was right. I knew she was onto something. I knew it was worth repeating. She was touching on a subject I had been grappling with but couldn't figure out how to succinctly and simply lean into it. Lori has immense talents and the highest EQ of anyone I know. She sees things I don't see at first. She understands people on a deep level. She is a truly exceptional mom and completely devoted to being home with our children as I served in public office for the better part of two decades. She juggled and managed and helped all of us get through our days and years with a skill I can't possibly describe here. Her super power was that she could see what we needed before we saw it; she listened better than anyone and could connect all of the dots. And that wasn't just true for our family. Her powers extended to everyone she'd meet—in a grocery store or in a school event. She always had a pulse on what people were dealing with and how they were feeling. This morning she was preaching in her own way from that special feel.

I left the house with a pad full of scribbles that all started off with "that's not freedom" in my suit pocket and hit the road en route to several stops that would end in Erie in this final swing before the primary.

A few days later, I was backstage for the Erie Democratic dinner. It was the kind of event that I've been to a million versions of before: a big space with a stage in the front of the room, buffet tables scattered with hulking chafing trays. It wasn't fancy, but it was packed, filled with passionate people from the local Democratic committee and local elected officials and candidates for office. While I was unopposed in the primary, each of the Democratic candidates for US Senate was there, including the eventual winner, John Fetterman, whom I spoke to briefly backstage. Days later he'd have a stroke that would sideline him for months of his campaign. I was minutes away from going on stage in front of hundreds of important people, days away from the primary.

"Hey," I whispered to Dana Fritz, who was running the campaign and now serves as my chief of staff, and Will Simons, my communications director. "I'm not giving my usual speech. How about we take *freedom* out for a spin?"

There was some unease from my team about doing something different at this stage in the race. But Lori's words at the breakfast table had hung with me all week and in between other events I worked through those thoughts with Dana. She's where I go when I need a gut check. When I need to figure something out. The person in my ear who I hear from last, right before a decision is made. She's been my right hand for a long time, and there's no one I trust more in my professional life. Over the course of then ten years, two different elected offices, and now running my campaign for Governor, she earned the right. She also knew that I very rarely gave a speech off notes, let alone a teleprompter, so this wasn't completely uncharted. But we were on the one-yard line that night. There was very little reason to rock the boat at that point. We just needed to get out the vote. But we also thought freedom should be on the ballot.

Lori's words from the breakfast table were in my ear.

I started off on stage hitting my usual points, but I quickly launched into our thoughts about freedom—about how ticked off I was by Republicans who loved to talk a big game about freedom, but that it's not freedom to tell our children what books they're allowed to read. It's not freedom to tell women what they can do with their bodies. It's not freedom to tell you that you can work, but you can't join a union. I added: And it sure as hell isn't freedom to say you can go vote, but they get to pick the winners. That's not freedom.

The whole energy of the room shifted. From where I was standing, I could see people lean in. They were nodding their heads and whispering to one another. Something was clicking, in them and in me. Will smiled when I came backstage after the speech. We took freedom out for a spin, and folks felt it.

I called Lori when I got into the truck that night to go to the next stop to tell her that she was right. She had no idea what I was talking about. Since our talk at the breakfast table, she'd since moved on to the complexities of her days, wrangling our kids and schedules while I was on the road, while I was obsessively thinking about how to make this a central argument on the campaign.

Democrats are the party of freedom—the freedom to come to this country and to build a future for your family, the freedom to choose your own health care and actually be able to afford it, to worship how you want to worship and to love whom you want to love. And yet Republicans—particularly the sort of candidate I was getting ready to run against for Governor—talked a big game about being the party of liberty while actually restricting freedom at every turn. I wasn't willing to cede that territory.

For the next couple of months, I included this theme in nearly every speech. Internally, some on my team were less confident that the message would land. I knew they weren't wrong, that talk about democracy and freedom might not resonate—especially in the face of rising costs, which remained the primary focus of my campaign. But I had this nagging sense that I couldn't shake, and kept coming back to, sometimes a dozen times a day. I knew that the talk of freedom should be hopeful and aspirational, not purely negative and focused on what the Republicans were doing wrong. That was lazy. Because there was some cause for hope with all of this. I just needed to find the light.

I called Pastor Mitchell on the way to what felt like my millionth stop during that campaign haul. "I think you need to look at Jesus's brothers, Paul and James," he said. "Paul, who wrote the bulk of the New Testament, says I am a Jew among Jews. Ain't nobody more Jewish than I am. Here are all the things that make me Jewish and the ways you need to practice your faith. This is what real religion is."

He pointed me to James 1:27. "Religion that G-d our Father accepts as pure and faultless is this: to look after orphans and widows in their distress and to keep oneself from being polluted by the world."

Real religion is actually that act of moving toward hard places and people in need, not away from them. It's not creating a new religion as much as it is reforming an old faith. "Dude," Marshall said. "You are doing that. This is what you live. That's real politics the way James talks about real religion. This is how you need to talk about real freedom—the ways in which you are bearing it out."

Now that got me thinking. That's always how I tried to live. That is how I served, how my faith weaves through me and my family. This was why I was running in the first place.

This was a way to articulate that. What struck me was that James wasn't tearing down the other way to do religion, which has its place and its followers. He was affirming his way, illuminating a new path, with hope, yes, but grounded in the work. Roots and wings. It wasn't enough to just be against the old way of doing things or the adulterated patriotism that many of the Republicans had claimed. Being opposed to something but for nothing of your own isn't enough. Opposition isn't enough to vote for or stand on. You need an affirmative. That's what I wanted to offer.

That's how my friend Pastor Marshall Mitchell helped me turn the germ of an idea that Lori planted into the fruits of a speech cultivated by my excellent team just days before the general election, at a rally in North Philadelphia 400 miles away from that stage in Erie and 165 days later. I was alongside Presidents Biden and Obama. There were seventy-five hundred people in the crowd. In a matter of days, democracy would be on the line.

I started by talking about Doug Mastriano, my then-opponent, a Trump acolyte who proudly participated in the January 6 insurrection. If you don't think like him, look like him, vote like him, worship like him, marry like him, you don't count in his Pennsylvania, I said. I know that because I know where he was on January 6. He went there that day to stop your vote from being counted because he doesn't respect you. He already told you that he's going to use his power as Governor to decertify certain voting machines in Pennsylvania, so he gets to pick the winner.

That is not how our democracy works. That's not how we do things in this Commonwealth or in this country. That is not freedom.

Then I went to the James of it all.

Here's what I told them: We are for real freedom. Real freedom is when you see the potential in a young child in North Philadelphia so you invest in her public school. That is real freedom. Real freedom comes when we invest in that young child's neighborhood to make sure that it's safe, so she gets to her eighteenth birthday. That's real freedom. Real freedom comes when we put technology in her schools and open up her eyes to the possibility of being a welder and send her to a union apprenticeship program and believe in her so she starts a small business right here in North Philadelphia. That is real freedom. Real freedom comes when she hires a whole bunch of people that were never going to have a shot before. They go on to marry the people they love, worship how they want, live in a community that is safe, live in a place that respects them.

★   ★   ★

I thought about that speech, how Pastor Mitchell and the people closest to me helped pull that out of me, as I walked to the front of his church that Sunday morning two weeks after the arson attack. I knew that I was going to be called upon to do something. I knew that I was going to recount the events of the last few weeks, because I owed it to these people, who had been praying for me and my family, who were there for us in this time of need and for many years before that. And I wanted to share it with them, because I needed help making sense of it myself. I needed to draw on some of their strength in that sunlit church with little halos of light dancing around the room. Rays were streaming through the windows that lined the back wall of the church. That's where all the light gets in.

As I stood before them, I explained that I wanted to be there that morning. That I needed to be there. That Salem Baptist Church was a place that has always helped me find comfort and direction and purpose, and I needed a little bit of that. I told them about what had happened—not so much about the facts surrounding the attack but more about how it made us feel. I told them about the fire department chaplain who had given me the prayer. I talked about how that struck me and stuck with me because of something I learned at this church during more than two decades of coming here: to be open to people of all different faiths and beliefs and walks of life to help center you, and to understand our shared and common humanity.

I told them that my family and I will be stronger from this.

We will not be deterred from our call to service and from practicing our faith openly and proudly. I wanted them to know I'm working my tail off for them every single day. That I was aware that right now there are a whole lot of people out there who are worried, who are scared, who are wondering if this is the nation that we worked so hard to build when things are now being taken away from us. The beautiful diversity of not just people but opinion and thought and faith that fills this church every Sunday to worship collectively and then go act in our communities on Monday.

I reminded them that we have a responsibility to do this work. That this church has always been a guiding light in making progress in our communities. The priest or pastor may have changed some of the window dressing, but the sunlight was shining in.

That light was on us right now, certainly on me, not just to appreciate the prayers, the common humanity, the goodness of people, but to use that energy, that goodness, that focus to push back on the negative and the chaos and to allow ourselves to continue to make progress.

*   *   *

Progress without chaos. That was swimming around my head as I took my seat back in my pew in the second row behind the deacons and deaconesses for Pastor Mitchell's sermon. He pointed us to the twenty-first chapter of John, verses five and six. Jesus said to them, "Children, do you have any fish?" They answered him, "No." He said to them, "Cast the net on the right side of the boat, and you will find some." So they cast it, and now they were not able to haul it in, because of the quantity of fish.

"I'd like to raise for just a few minutes the topic of fishing differently," Pastor Mitchell said. What worked in the past, he told us, will not work in the future. If we keep fishing on the side of the boat where we lost, we will remain losers. It was not a call for us to abandon the core tenets and principles of our faith, but a cry and a call for us to look to new things and to do things differently.

Toward the end of his message, he called on me directly in my pew.

"Keep fishing differently," he said.

I have fished differently my entire life. Throughout my career, I have been fortunate enough to have considered opportunities along what would be a conventional political path, from the halls of Congress to the short list for the vice presidency. These would have raised my profile and allowed me to work on behalf of more people. The political establishment told me I'd be crazy not to take them. But I didn't take the conventional path.

I tell my children all the time that conventional wisdom is never really all that wise. If you are firm enough in your convictions and your reasons why, then you will always end up in your right place. What is right for you might not be right for the people urging you to do their right thing. In order to feel what my right is, I have to return to my center.

I didn't start out in public service with the goal of becoming Governor or working in Washington. My calling was to serve in a way where I could still be a great father and husband, to serve in a way where I could be impactful and actually get shit done.

When I got my start, it didn't feel like it feels today. For many years, decades even, you may not have agreed with the people in power, but they were respectful and respectable, decent and did the right thing. They tried their best to solve problems. And, for many of us, it worked. We felt we were better off than our parents and had opportunities to give our children better lives than we had.

Over the last number of years, that sentiment has changed. Rightly so. Wages stagnated. The housing market crashed. There is a crisis of affordability, a lack of mobility, uncertainty around a future where AI could dominate and revolutionize, a mounting pressure on the middle class, and high-stakes tests on civic norms upon which this country was built. People felt more isolated, prospects slimmer. Overregulation got in the way of growth. Drugs and guns filled our streets while jobs went overseas because of lopsided trade deals in the nineties that hurt my state especially. Higher education and some CEOs thumbed their nose at real people, doing real work, trying to build real futures for their families. Both parties stopped hearing each other. The dialogue diminished. Anger raged.

That is how you got the rise of someone like President Donald Trump, who fed off this feeling that the government isn't working for regular people. His entire message is built around resentment, around going backward, around creating false enemies and blaming others. His approach is to attack institutions, to do away with norms, to go after marginalized people in this country, and then present himself as the only savior. Politics of grievance.

There is so much to legitimately fear and loathe and resist about what we have witnessed in this era of politics. That's why I sued the first Trump administration dozens of times in my time as Attorney General. On election results, process, and voting rights alone, we sued them more than forty times, and we won every one of them. But while I had profound differences with the guy, and I didn't like the way he talked, and I certainly didn't like the values and viewpoints he espoused, I only sued his administration when I believed that he was actually violating the law. I didn't join every lawsuit that every Attorney General in every state brought against him just because I knew it would make for a good headline or get attention on social media.

That's why I won the lion's share of the challenges I brought against them. Because we were rooted in the law, not politics. And it's why I continue to show up in districts and cities and towns where I know people support him. Maybe they voted for me or maybe they didn't. It doesn't matter much—I'm fishing differently. I will show up for people who like him and work my butt off for them the way I'd do for anyone in the great Commonwealth of Pennsylvania. I'll help them and hear them and do the work required of me.

We can't oppose everything he does just because we don't like the guy.

In order to effectively fight for what we believe in, we need to provide an alternative that actually works. It is not slashing and burning, but building and generating. To have the future we want, we need to create more of what we need. And in order to know what we need, we have to show up in our communities. We need to listen to our neighbors. We need to be for something—not just against everything.

It may not be popular to say right now, but I believe in government. I always have. I believe that it can be a force for good in people's lives. Now, if you're going to run for office, you inherently believe that the system has purpose, otherwise you would take your talents elsewhere and maybe make some money and age more gracefully along the way. That doesn't mean I think the way in which it is functioning right now is working. We have real, serious work to do across all of these areas. That work is going to require sacrifice and openness to change.

What it doesn't require is a wrecking ball. We need new bricks. We need to invest in what's good, divest from what's not.

Fish differently.

This is already playing out across America, in places I get the privilege of going to every day, where I get a glimpse into how people across the country are actually putting this into practice. Being in these places, it is so clear to me that there is a glaring disconnect between what's coming out of DC and from some in the media and what is actually happening on the ground in these communities every day. The privilege of what we do is that we get to go out into these communities and see neighbors selflessly helping neighbors, people working to better the lives of strangers. No one asks if you are a Republican or Democrat or who you voted for before they get to work solving problems and lending hands.

I could rattle off a million examples. On any given evening, as Lori and I sit down to go through our day, she will tell me about people like Tristan and Emerson Rankin, brothers who, as high school students, started Coats of Friendship, a nonprofit in York, Pennsylvania, which collects coats, hats, and gloves for people in need. In 2024 alone, they gave out ten thousand coats to law enforcement and first responders and volunteer firefighters and neighbors of theirs in need. Or Jared Quinteros, whom she met as she saw his artwork on display at the University of Pittsburgh Medical Center (UPMC). Jared tragically lost his wife and the mother of their two sons, Kara Leo, in the summer of 2021 on a hike in Upper St. Clair, when a tree limb fell on both of them. He broke his back and lost the ability to walk. As he worked through his grief and learned to navigate the world differently, he turned to art as an outlet and way to heal. He now volunteers at UPMC, teaching newly injured patients to rebuild their lives and work through their pain through art.

Lori and I could tell you about Denise O'Connor, who founded the Mid-Atlantic Mothers' Milk Bank in Pittsburgh, an organization that sources and supplies safe, ethically collected donor breast milk for babies in medical need in Pennsylvania. She works tirelessly to make sure that every vulnerable infant has access to the nutrients they need, growing the organization to supply forty thousand ounces of donor milk each month to eighty-two hospitals and dozens of outpatient facilities.

The antidote to all the fear and division is these people. It's their community connection. It's their selflessness. And it's happening in communities all over the place. You may not read about it on X or hear about it from the Briefing Room in the White House right now. But it's all around us. We just need to look for that light. I feel blessed that I have the opportunity to see it, and the ability to then try to further this good work.

I have made choices throughout my career to figure out new ways to make people's lives a little better. Frankly, it isn't all that complicated to actually deliver real things to real people that matter to them, even if our politics don't always align. What we need to do is meet people where they are. Understand what they need. And then do the hard work to connect the dots, form the partnerships, and bring people together to make their lives better. That's it.

What do you need?

How can we help?

How can we get this done?

You show up, even for people who didn't vote for you.

You listen, even if you don't agree 100 percent of the time. Maybe even especially when you don't.

You talk to them with respect. You feel empathy for what they are facing.

That is the soul work, the service.

This is the basic lesson I learned twenty years ago knocking on eighteen thousand doors in the community I grew up in, on my way to an improbable victory for state representative in a district that had voted Republican for two decades before I decided to run.

CHAPTER II

18,000 Doors

IF I AM BEING TOTALLY honest, I had no idea if it was going to work. When I was in elementary school, I had started writing letters to Avi Goldstein, a Jewish boy just a little bit younger than me who was living in Tbilisi, USSR, and trying to immigrate to Israel. The idea came from my mom, who was a teacher in her previous life and now a stay-at-home mom to my brother, sister, and me while deeply involved in the Soviet Jewry movement. She helped connect young Americans with "refuseniks," who were Jewish Soviet citizens who were refused permission to emigrate by the communist government. As my mom's eldest, I was drafted right away. There were boys just like me, she'd tell me, who couldn't openly celebrate Shabbat every Friday night like we did as a family or go to a Jewish school like my siblings and I did, who didn't have nearly any of the freedoms I definitely took for granted.

My dad was the local pediatrician who just about everyone leaned on. He had his own private practice and also worked out of a public health clinic in Norristown, a neighborhood not like the one we lived in, to serve a community that needed doctors like him. Between his private practice that he was building and his clinic work, he was always on call or doing rounds, bringing my siblings and me with him regularly. Anytime anyone would ask what we wanted to be when we grew up, I vividly remember saying that I wanted to be the guy everybody calls when they have a problem—just like my dad.

So that's why as an elementary schooler I was happy to oblige when my mom told me she wanted me to write letters to a boy I didn't know, who lived in the Soviet Union, which, to me, might as well have been the moon.

I was decidedly not a star student in elementary school. It is family lore that after one act of harmless misbehavior—of which there were many—my parents were called into the principal's office. Her name was Mrs. Landes, and she was so extremely tall and her office so extremely tiny that when you were in there, you had the distinct feeling of being in a dollhouse. I'd momentarily locked a classmate of mine in a teacher's supply closet. Momentarily! I let him right out. But not before lightly jamming his finger in the door. I—rightly—wound up in that dollhouse of an office, with Mrs. Landes telling me this was the final straw, and that I had two choices: I could either take a suspension, or I could get my act together.

I chose the latter, obviously, and I shaped up. My parents got the brunt of it.

"Your son," she told them, "is either going to find a lot of trouble, or he is going to be very, very successful." Let the record show that she once said the same thing about her own son, I am told.

I didn't have my sights set on either of those two options. Mostly, I just wanted to watch the Sixers and play basketball. But I felt a calling to be in the mix, in the energy around other people. I knew that however it came up, and it very often did, that I just wanted to be the guy with the ball.

And so I was game to continue writing my pen pal, though it was usually one-sided. Every month, my mom would write her own letters to refusenik families, and I would sit down and write mine to Avi. I'd tell him what my school was like, or talk about a Philadelphia sports team. I rarely heard back, because the Soviet government would usually intercept Avi's letters, but that wasn't the point, my mom would explain. She assured me that at the very least, my letters would brighten Avi's day, and at best, maybe it could help bring him and his family to safety.

I didn't know it then, but Avi very much needed that. For more than a decade, Avi's family had been seeking permission to leave the Soviet Union for Israel. The family had become used to their apartment being searched and relatives being sent to prison because of their faith. As a result, they pulled Avi from school around the time I started writing him to keep him safe through homeschooling. When his parents decided to send him to school for sixth grade, he proudly shared with his new classmates that he was Jewish. Their response was to beat him so brutally that he suffered a traumatic brain injury and had to remain home for three months. When he did return, despite the school's guarantee that it would never happen again, a half dozen of his classmates grabbed him, stripped off his clothes, and took a picture of his circumcision. Avi had written me back detailing all of this, but only some of his letters got to me, which was the result of Soviet censors.

By the time I was getting ready for my Bar Mitzvah—a Jewish rite of passage that marks a young man's entry into adulthood around his thirteenth birthday—my mom and I started a national group called Children for Avi to get as many people as we could to write letters on his behalf. I wanted him and his family to be able to flee this persecution and to make it to Israel. My hope was that after they got to safety in Israel, he would be able to come to America and finally meet me in person.

The group grew to dozens of people writing to him and on his behalf. My mom organized a trip to Washington, DC, where we got to sit down with Senator Arlen Specter and then-Senator Joe Biden among others to lobby for Avi and the other kids.

This is not the point in the story where I reveal that this was my aha moment where I saw my destiny to work in politics unfurl before me as a preteen.

I didn't know much about these senators at the time and didn't really understand what they did. I knew they seemed influential. I saw that they had fancy offices and wore full suits and ties. I knew that they had the ability to get something done for us. That government could be a positive force in people's lives. What did appeal to me was that I saw that if you were active and engaged, if you stuck to something and worked at it and fought to have your voice heard on something you believed to be right, then some good could eventually come. I saw that service could lead to action, that one boy writing letters could turn into dozens of kids writing letters, which could lead to these people in these fancy offices, in their suits and ties, actually effecting change. The power of that domino effect stuck with me.

Eventually, Avi's story reportedly reached the desk of Senator Ted Kennedy, who made a request to then–Soviet leader Mikhail Gorbachev that the family be permitted to finally leave for freedom in Israel. Five weeks before my Bar Mitzvah, Soviet authorities agreed.

It was May 1986 when I got up on the bimah—the pulpit—at Beth Sholom in Elkins Park, the historic Frank Lloyd Wright–designed synagogue where my family went nearly every Saturday morning for Shabbat through my whole childhood, where my folks and our family still go to this day.

Avi stood by my side.

We had met for the first time the day before, and now here we were, standing in front of hundreds of people who came to mark this moment with us. He didn't speak much English and had never seen a Torah—the holy scrolls that contain the five books of the Bible, held sacred in synagogues—but he chanted the blessings in Hebrew perfectly before I read from the Torah for the first time. After I finished, I told the congregation just how much it meant to share that moment with him, how I really never expected that our work would pay off. "I thought I would have to symbolically share this with him," I said. I added that I was worried about the thousands of other Jewish kids still in the Soviet Union who weren't freely living out their faith as we now were. My work, I told them, wasn't done.

Rabbi Aaron Landes—who not so coincidentally was married to Mrs. Landes, the tall principal from my school—told the crowd there that morning that I had a "special dignity that is reflective of a young man with a purpose, a goal."

At the time, I was hoping that my former principal might be there to hear those words, because maybe they'd buy me a little bit of grace from her. Now, they mean more than just about anything.

The story got coverage in local news, and I started traveling around the country to give speeches for different organizations about our advocacy. I got a feel for speaking in public and figured out pretty early on that I liked engaging with people. I had prepared notes, but I felt comfortable talking off the cuff about the things that mattered to me in front of people to whom I knew those things mattered, too.

What made those trips more special was that I'd get to go with my dad. He was working so hard and so much at the time that getting these concentrated pockets of uninterrupted time together felt special. I still think about our trip to Cleveland, when the group that had brought me in had sent a limousine to pick us up from the airport. Obviously, it was my first time in a limo, and it felt like something out of a movie or a dream.

Avi went on to have his own Bar Mitzvah in Israel and years later became a tenured mathematics professor at the City University of New York and an ordained rabbi at Yeshiva University. After a few years, we didn't really keep in touch, and I haven't seen him since. For me, I would later realize that these were the moments that helped lead me into a life of faith and public service.

*   *   *

The house where Lori and I have lived for more than two decades is about a ten-minute drive from my childhood home, a corner house on Dundee Drive and Burn Brae Drive, at the intersection of middle-class suburban life. We moved there in June 1979, just after I turned six. I was born in Kansas City, where my dad was in medical school. I don't remember living in Kansas City and eventually rooted hard against the Chiefs when they played the Eagles in the Super Bowls, but I do remember little snippets of those early years here and there.

After completing medical school in Kansas City, we moved to the Philadelphia area, where my dad did his internship and residency from 1974 to 1977 at the Naval Regional Medical Center in Philadelphia. We then moved to Naval housing on a military base called Mitchel Field on Long Island until 1979. My father completed his two years of active duty there while we lived in officers' quarters. He wore a white uniform to work, and I thought there was just nothing cooler. Expect for maybe the stories I got to hear about life on a submarine.

After his naval commitment ended, we settled in Upper Dublin, about eight miles from Philadelphia. My dad opened his private practice in 1980, which he ran until he sold it just a couple of years ago. My parents bought a four-bedroom house and filled it with three kids. I am the oldest, followed three years later by my sister, Rebecca, and three years after that, by my brother, Adam. We had a hoop in the driveway where we'd obsessively play basketball. I was a pitcher in our Little League and practiced a ton. My dad used to be a catcher, and he would crouch down next to a tree in the yard that mimicked the batter. I pitched over and over to him. He taught me how to throw a mean split-fingered fastball by that tree. There was a park across the street where everyone in the neighborhood gathered to hit baseballs or throw footballs. I rode my BMX everywhere. The older kids in the neighborhood would babysit us, until we became the bigger kids, and then we'd babysit for the microgeneration below us. I hung posters of Dr. J and Michael Jordan on the wall behind my bed in my room. When I got a bit older, a poster of Heather Locklear found its way onto my wall, too. (Those posters, minus Ms. Locklear's, are hanging in our son Reuben's bedroom to this day.)

My brother's bedroom and mine shared a wall. After lights out, my AM/FM radio was tuned to 610 AM to listen to sports radio, and we'd bang on the shared drywall in a secret code. My sister had the big bedroom across the hall. The three of us were an inseparable trio, a triangle filled with love and affection all the closeness you could ever hope for in your siblings. We played together constantly, mainly outside or in the basement where we had a TV, a Ping-Pong table, a bunch of games, and some gymnastics equipment on which Rebecca, a great gymnast, practiced for hours. At her meets, I was tasked with recording her performances with our massive VHS camcorder so she could watch them later. I try to avoid mentioning the one time I "accidentally" recorded an important episode of *Miami Vice* over the footage I'd caught of her championship meet.

My brother and I used her mats to wrestle and play a football game where we would put the football in the middle of the mat, yell hike, race toward the middle, collide, then have to drag the football and the other person back to our own end zone. Rebecca generally tolerated this, apart from the one time when I managed to twist Adam's neck while fighting for the ball. He ended up missing a week of camp while recovering. To this day I feel awful for the way I hurt him.

There was a local elementary school just up the road where we had a bunch of friends and played pickup games, but we went to the Forman Hebrew Day School about ten minutes from our house. Every Friday night, our family had Shabbat dinner at home, just the five of us. On Saturday mornings, we went to synagogue. I would have rather spent those weekend mornings sleeping in or playing ball with the other kids in my neighborhood. But there was something to the routine of it, the community around these rituals that grounded me, even as I complained about getting dragged out of bed and putting on my dress shirt and uncomfortable dress shoes on a Saturday.

We didn't spend much time with our grandparents. Both of my parents had strained relationships with their parents and families. They'd grown up close by in West Oak Lane, a nice neighborhood in Philadelphia where most of their friends were from. We did spend a bunch of time with my folks' friends from their childhoods. We had our neighbors. We had our school community and our synagogue. Because my dad treated so many families in town, I always felt at the center of our little universe. Everyone knew him. They'd call our house at all hours of the night, and he would answer every parent with such calm and wisdom and patience. I remember him listening more than talking, even though he'd dealt with every version of a stomach bug or fever that each panicked parent would call asking about.

"What do you think, Mom?" he'd ask them. "You are the mom, you know your child best," he would say.

It would drive these frantic parents crazy, I'm sure. As a dad, I know that in these moments all you want is answers, a road map. I reflect on that question all the time now as someone who serves his community in a very different capacity, but as a leader people count on for answers. What my dad knew is that your gut is often your best bet in leading you to what's right, and the power of being heard is just as important as the peace in being told. That always stuck with me.

*　*　*

My mom is a woman of purpose, of service, of kindness and good. She and my dad met when they were in high school, and she went on to teach elementary school in the Philadelphia public school system before they moved to Kansas City for my dad's medical training. She stayed at home with my siblings and me until she went back to teaching when we were teenagers, volunteering at our school doing social action work and making sure that we completed the tasks our faith and our family values called on us to do. She was particularly involved as a national leader in the Soviet Jewry movement—helping those refuseniks like Avi. She used that sense of advocacy to draw in students like my classmates, my siblings, and me to help us find our voices and our power to help others. I really looked forward to the days when my mom would come to school and spend time with my classmates, teaching us, empowering us, and inspiring us to help others. Her standards were high and her sense of duty greater. She would write weekly newsletters that detailed the progress we were helping to make and all that was left to accomplish. She'd write it all by hand, because, not to date myself, this was pre–word processor. There was no task she wasn't willing to do, no person she wasn't willing to help or convince to lend a hand. She led. She taught. She felt compelled and connected to the cause. She put in the work. From her, I witnessed what true activism looked like, that it takes time and real dedication. That it doesn't happen overnight but that you can't be deterred by setbacks and slowdowns. That if something was worth fighting for, you had to take all the steps, weather the storms, put in the time. That we were here to do good in the world, to do the right thing with our voices for those who weren't able to speak up for themselves.

I was really proud that she was my mom, particularly when she worked in our school. She had this uncommon gift as an extraordinary teacher and mentor. I saw how preternaturally present and thoughtful and sweet and loving she was to her students and in the community. I certainly took all of those things with me, and carried them in to my own understanding of what it meant to lead and how to serve.

And as much as I respected how she showed up, I was also bewildered by it. Because the person that she was as a teacher and pillar in the community was sometimes different from the one I knew at home.

This is not something I have talked much about, even privately, but certainly not publicly. Part of that is because I have not felt like the story is mine to share. I haven't come to the decision lightly, to write about it like this. It's something I've debated, gone back and forth about, tossed and turned over. It is my truth, my lived experience.

The way I understand it, my mom grew up unsafe in her extremely unstable childhood home. She had no full siblings and a father who left when she was just two. She lived with her mother and a series of stepfathers over the years and was never supported or cared for the way all children deserve to be. I think it's fair to say that both my parents, for very different reasons, suffered trauma and dysfunction from how they grew up, and that shaped them into who they became as adults, partners, and parents. Those traumas certainly shaped how they interacted with each other and ultimately with my siblings and me.

It eats away at me, just knowing that the events of my mom's childhood caused her to struggle throughout. She grew up in an era when therapy was taboo and mental health issues came with a real stigma. Getting help and talking about these struggles were certainly not recognized and talked about the way they are today. She gritted through a lot without actually dealing with or talking through it. We all did. I don't want to make it seem like there wasn't joy and stability and safety in our family. There was. We had so much good fortune. We loved each other. Rebecca and Adam and I were always incredibly close, as we remain today. They're such central relationships and guideposts for me, in a way that siblings can only hope to be. We were safe, cared for. Our needs were beyond met. But two things can be true: I had a happy childhood and, at points, an unhappy childhood home.

At a young age, I knew how to spot a brewing problem from a mile away, almost instinctively. My siblings and I thought that if we were good, we could stop the chaos and the yelling and keep a sense of calm for my mom and the house overall. This instability consumed us all, though I tried to shield Adam and Rebecca from as much of it as I could.

The pressure of it all had a way of seeping into the cracks and corners of my life. While it brought my siblings and me closer, it isolated me outside of the people who lived within our four walls. I felt like there was a huge part of my life that I couldn't share with others. I was embarrassed by it. I never brought other kids over to play inside for fear of what they might see or hear.

I know that what I am describing is a reality that many people understand—what it's like to witness someone they love so much struggle, how those struggles tend to bleed into and tug at those around them. To not share this would ignore the fact that mental health is something that most families grapple with but so few feel comfortable talking about. And if I avoided talking about the topic, I would be leaving out the piece of me that has influenced basically every part of my life and who I am as well as the complexities that come from growing up this way. I love my mom more than anything. I worry about her. I want her to find joy and see her many blessings, chief among them ten incredible grandchildren, and not be consumed by the darkness that traps her at times.

I can trace many decisions I've made, the soft spots I protect, the way I move through the world and manner in which I lead to growing up in the midst of my mom's challenges. It explains why I sought a path that would give me control and autonomy, because once I left my house, I vowed that I would never be back there again—and I basically never was. I loved my brother and sister and folks so much and wanted to be around them, but I also knew how the environment would make me feel. It explains why I always sought to solve problems, because as a kid that's just what I was trained to do. I had to anticipate a problem or a pain point before there was a blowup. I knew how to find a solution, and quick, so I could avoid a meltdown at home. It explains not only why I feel so deeply for the underdog and people taken advantage of, but why it pains me so much to see how the families of victims and of those struggling are impacted by these struggles. It explains the kind of husband I am, the sort of father I try to be, because I never wanted Lori or my kids to experience one second of what I sometimes lived through—the chaos, the yelling, the tiptoeing around.

I sought out the comfort in feeling like I was in charge of something, that I was in control and in command in a way that I never quite felt like I had at home. Those breaks, I found, brought me such relief. I'd only really ever known the opposite.

Until I met Lori.

While I'd been at my school since the seventh grade, Lori started in ninth grade at Akiba Hebrew Academy for high school.

My immediate reaction was just about exactly what you would expect from a teenage boy. Well, I thought, she's really cute and fun and I am definitely going to flirt with her. We became friends, long before anything else. I would take the SEPTA train from North Hills to Langhorne, where her mom would pick me up at the train station. Her house became a haven for me. Her mom Ellie loved to cook. She had recently divorced from her first husband John, an engineer, and remarried, Saul, the local veterinarian. Everyone got along and even had family meals together. There were always people coming in and out. No one yelled, at all. People disagreed and got frustrated with each other, but they didn't raise their voices. Witnessing that kind of conflict resolution and communication unlocked something in me. In all the many conflicts that have come up as we've grown together, the millions of hard moments big and small that you face in a marriage and as parents and now, as public servants, we don't raise our voices. In my time in her house and in getting to see how she navigated the world, how her family all communicated how they felt with such kindness and respect and measure, I found what I lacked. I was not going to repeat the same patterns. Not as a partner, nor as a parent. Lori showed me a different path, what that could look and feel like, at a young enough age that it totally changed how I communicate and compose myself.

We were pretty immediately inseparable. We would go off campus to the local deli to have cheese fries for lunch, which is how you know it was getting pretty serious. But, officially, we were just friends until our junior year of high school, when we started dating in earnest.

At Akiba, the junior class gets to spend the first semester in Israel—from Labor Day until New Year's. It is three dozen eleventh-graders living in a dorm all together, going to a few hours of classes every day, and traveling as a group with lots of time to hang out and experience life in Israel. Until then, the only trips I'd ever been on were some summer weeks in Ocean City, Maryland, and a few places here and there—like to Cooperstown to visit the Baseball Hall of Fame, a visit to Maine, and those speaking engagements with my dad. But there I was, sixteen years old in Jerusalem for four months, with Lori and all of my buddies. We toured all around. She was my best friend, and we were exploring this country that felt like magic to me. Now, obviously, we were in Jewish Day School. Heading into that trip, I connected to my faith within the four walls of my house on a Friday night or the four walls of my synagogue on a Saturday morning. It was very regimented and structured. But there was something foundational about being in Israel that really connected me more to my faith. In

Israel, it was just everywhere. It was the first time I could feel faith. I could see it and touch it and it wasn't abstract. It was in front of me, in the middle of the desert. It was around me on a Saturday evening, after sundown on Shabbat, as we went to Ben-Yehuda Street. It's a cobblestone street on a hill that's teeming with crowds and filled with life, where people spill out of restaurants and bars, music plays, young Israelis and visitors meet up with friends. It's particularly vibrant after Shabbat, since everything closes from Friday into Saturday, and many people are with their families observing the day of rest. Nearly every time we'd go, I would run into someone I knew or who knew someone I knew, or was from Pennsylvania or had some connection to my family or my friends. We were halfway across the world and there we were, bound by this tie, by this place, brought together by our Judaism, by our past and our present and our presence. In that, I found a deeper meaning of faith.

I really felt it when we went to the Western Wall for the first time. It was during the High Holy Days—the period marking the Jewish New Year and our day of repentance. I wore baggy khakis that had about eight thousand pleats—it was the nineties!—and a white short-sleeved button down, which were definitely the nicest clothes that I had. We had walked there as a group, the same people I had spent a decade in class studying Hebrew and talking about the Torah with, learning about the history of this city and the significance of this Wall. Most of our education and time in the classroom had been centered around our religion, and here we were, together, taking it in. It was not just a lesson, it was a moment in life. To do that with them felt almost surreal, almost too big and too great.

We had prepared notes to slip into the wall's cracks, as is tradition. Usually you write a prayer or wish or something you want to convey to G-d. I wish I could remember what mine said, but I do remember putting my hand on the Wall. It was cool and worn, like you could feel the millions of hands that had been placed there before you. My faith in that moment was around me. I was touching it. I was breathing it. My faith was alive and its roots grew deeper under me.

*   *   *

The semester in Israel flew by. I loved every minute of it. Once we returned home in January 1990, I ran for my first political position as student body president. It remains the only race I have lost in my career. I am twelve and one thus far, which sounds pretty good until you realize that that one, singular loss was a complete and total massacre. I got creamed. I don't remember much about my platform, but I think I promised more soda in the vending machines or something. Ami Eden won. Hannah Richman was a close second. Me, a very, very, all-the-way-down-the-field distant third. In all likelihood, I was probably less interested in the role than I was in impressing Lori, so I can't say that I was exactly crushed by the defeat. When people ask her whether she always knew that I would be in politics or if this was my clear destiny, Lori gamely points them to this experience as her answer.

I was more successful on the basketball court. In my senior year, we really clicked as a team. I'd grown up playing with all of the guys on our team, but this was the last dance. Two of them had just gone through a growth spurt and gotten super tall—a lucky fate that was not my own. The guy who'd beat me to become class president got tall enough that he could dunk, which I feel confident saying is the first and likely the last time in Akiba history that that has happened. I was the point guard, and the season started off a bit rocky, but we settled into a rhythm. We ripped off twenty-plus straight wins. I'd never felt a sense of camaraderie and teamwork like that before. We worked our asses off. No one was a selfish player. Our stat lines didn't matter to us. We just wanted to win, together.

I wasn't the best guy on the court. I didn't shoot as much as other starters, though it has to be said that I did contribute sixteen points in the championship game. I became known on the team as "The General," because I set the tone for the team when we were on the court. I called the plays and told my teammates where to be. I was usually able to see how things were going to play out on the court before they happened.

So while I couldn't dunk, and I wasn't the fastest runner, nor was I the person who could sink shots from half court or score the most points, I knew I could lead and create plays. And I wanted to. I always just wanted the ball in my hands. On the court and in my life and career. When there are two minutes left in the game, I want the ball in my hands and I want to call the play, because I have faith in my ability to see what's ahead, make the right move at the right time, and get others involved so they can be their best selves.

Now, that doesn't mean I don't fail. I am very comfortable with failure, and I will learn from it and not make that same mistake again. There is certainly a lot of pressure in this.

On our team today, we have a motto that we never grade against anyone else. Not another Governor, not another politician. We only grade against ourselves. And while we are constantly tweaking how we can improve our processes and decisions, the conclusion is never that we could have worked harder. Because I have always felt that I outworked every situation and everyone. There are definitely times when I could have done something a different way—and I want that feedback, internally or externally, so that I can do it better the next time—but I know that any loss or failure or mistake has not come as a result of not trying my hardest.

Even in the moments where we do get it right and get praise and feel good, we still ask ourselves whether we could have done something better. Could we have done it more efficiently? If someone writes or says something critical, as we look at how we handled it, if we felt we handled things as best as we could, we don't get down about the criticism. We're not looking to outsiders or the media for affirmation, nor are we overacting to criticism. We focus on acting with integrity, working hard, doing our best, and grading against ourselves, not someone else's standards.

My team, and Dana, in particular, anchors me in that constant self-assessing and questioning. It's something that just works for us, and something that fills us with a lot of pride.

All of that has come from me wanting the ball, just as I did my senior year of high school. I have just always trusted myself to know where and how and when to take the shot and handle the pressure, and I have always been willing to accept the miss. There is never not something to learn from a miss.

*　　*　　*

In the fall of 1991, I was ready to get to work. I sat down at the word processor in the library that evening anticipating that I was on the precipice of history. I was in the early days of my freshman year at the University of Rochester, relishing being on my own. After a disastrous roommate situation in the first few weeks of my freshman year—the guy unceremoniously threw all of my belongings out of the dorm window while I was at basketball practice for no apparent reason—I settled in. I was playing basketball and on the premed track, knowing that I wanted to follow in my dad's footsteps and help people in the same way he had.

Lori and I had broken up, though to this day I prefer to think of it as being on a break. She headed off to Colgate, which was only about two hours from Rochester—roughly the distance that I commute several times each week from our home in Abington to the state Capitol. But to us, as eighteen-year-olds, we might as well have had an ocean between us. We went our separate ways, hoping that we would figure it out down the road. At least I was hoping. But this was a breakup before iPhones, social media, email. Before cell phones, even. If we wanted to reach each other, we would have to pick up a landline, leave a message, wait for a call back.

Or, if you were me, and you wanted to really make a statement and set her world on fire, you could compose a letter that would make your one true love's heart beat out of her chest and send her across that ocean from one town in upstate New York to the other town in upstate New York to come see me. I missed her, more than I thought I would, and I knew just what to say to get her back. So I cracked my knuckles, and wrote my heart out. I was Shakespeare composing a sonnet. I was Taylor Swift before Taylor Swift. I was Lloyd Dobler in *Say Anything*, in a trench coat with the boom box over my head. I was getting the girl back. I talked about our roots, and how we were branches in a tree, forever intersecting and intertwined. It was magnificent. A work of art. Envelope. Stamp. Post office.

I envisioned that she would get the letter one night after she got home to her dorm. She would read it alone in her room, and be so moved that she would race down the hall out the door with her pajamas still on. She would drive through a rainstorm to get to me, because when you realize that you want to spend the rest of your life with someone, you want the rest of your life to start right now.

This, I am sorry to say, was not what played out. She never even responded to the letter. She did not write back. She did not call me. I didn't hear a single word from her until months later, when we were home over a break, when I had to ask her if she got it or if it had been lost in the mail (which was something my tortured, shattered spirit convinced myself might have happened). It had not been lost in the mail. She had received it and thought it was so dramatic and hilarious that she shared it with her roommate. Her roommate thought it was so dramatic and hilarious that she shared it with some others in their hall. And they all thought it was so dramatic and hilarious that they did a dramatic, hilarious reading of it for her dorm, crying with laughter over my every word.

Okay, so maybe I was a little purple with my prose. Needless to say, I realized it was probably time for me to move on, and definitely a reason for me to never show my face on Colgate's campus. To wit, when I joined Lori for her thirtieth reunion at Colgate—my first and only visit—in May 2025, some of those same friends could not hold themselves back from recounting the reading and calling me "Mr. Lori."

I thought for sure that would be the worst thing that could come my way during my first semester, but late into the fall just as the season was getting going, I got cut from the college basketball team.

I was crushed. I loved to play, of course, but I loved being part of the team even more. Basketball was a huge part of my identity and made up a gigantic portion of my new social life and community on campus. (It has to be noted that in the recent past, my friend Jay Wright, the championship winning Villanova coach, who was an assistant under Rochester basketball head coach Mike Neer the years before I got to campus, told Mike this story of how he cut the future Governor. Mike told Jay he actually remembered me and said in any other year I would have earned a spot on his squad except they were stacked that year. Okay, some small vindication thirty years later.)

It just so happened that on the very day I was cut, my premed professor called me into his office. Out of the 165-point exam he had given that week, I scored a 4. I studied hard. I didn't screw around. I was a serious student at that point. It just didn't click for me. I didn't like it. I couldn't begin to grasp it.

"I don't think this is for you," he said, meaning the premed track.

So I didn't have Lori. I couldn't hack it at basketball. And I was never going to be a doctor.

I called my dad when I was back in my dorm that evening. I am quite sure that I was dramatic about what felt like the biggest rainstorm on all of my parades at the same time. Nothing was turning out as I'd planned. Everything I wanted and everything that I had was slipping through my fingers. And, adding to all that misery and pressure and defeat, I couldn't stomach the idea that I would disappoint my dad. "Just be whatever it is that you want to be," he said. "You don't have to be a doctor. You just have to find the thing that makes you happy, and I don't think that being a doctor is your path to that."

So, some relief washed over me. But not enough. Now what am I going to do? I thought.

"Shapiro?" I heard a knock at my door that same evening. It was one of the guys who lived down the hall. "Have you ever thought about student senate? They need someone from our dorm and I heard you have the time."

*   *   *

I really had no interest, especially after that brutal high school election, but I did have the time. I had nothing to lose, and if I wasn't going to be a doctor—as that exam grade was proof of—then maybe this could be another way for me to serve. I don't want to pretend that I got it at that moment—hindsight is very helpful here. I knew then that I wasn't cut out for premed, but this part—the service part—I knew a little something about.

I liked the idea of needing to win.

I was open to taking the risk, to trying lots of different things. Especially since at that very moment, it felt like all my other doors had just slammed shut.

I say this to my own kids constantly or whenever I am in front of a group of young people: you never know what is going to strike a passion in you. I never thought about entering politics. The truth is, if you stay open to the bends in the road, to taking detours sometimes, to getting lost and then found and working hard throughout it all, that's when you end up where you were meant to be.

That was certainly the case with the student senate. I won the race. I got along with the other students involved and enjoyed the work that we got to do together. It just so happened that that semester the university's president had cut funding to club sports. So if I focused on this area for the senate, then I would not only be able to keep my connection to the athletic community, but I'd actually be able to make a difference and help them out. I could have my foot in both worlds.

And I was actually able to get stuff done. I organized a student protest against the funding cuts, worked with administrators, and ultimately was able to claw back a big chunk of money to support the athletes.

By second semester of my freshman year, I had switched my major to political science. The race for student association president had just heated up. There were others who had already declared they were running, all of them juniors, which would make them president in their senior year. That was how it always was. Until that year, when I decided to throw my freshman hat into the ring. Why not?

That April, *The Campus Times*, the student newspaper, ran a spread featuring each of the six candidates, myself included, where we laid out our vision for our terms as president. I wrote, "As a freshman, I have learned how to listen to your needs and desires and cultivate that input into concrete ideas, goals, and in the end—results. I have grown this year through meeting and discussing the issues with as many of you as I have been able to. This growing-up process has included so many of you, in both the academic field and the social field, and has made me discover just how special the U of R and its student body really is."

Clearly, what I lacked in actual wisdom, I made up for with my earnestness and self-seriousness. I can feel my kids' embarrassment for me reading this (if they ever read this, which they have sworn to never do).

I made some promises about handling faculty cuts and strengthening the requirements for teaching assistants. I knocked on what felt like every dorm room door on campus.

I made myself known. I listened to what my fellow students wanted.

I won the race. It was the first time in school history a freshman had ever done so, kicking off a long tradition of me being the youngest guy in the room and me doing a lot of things that everyone would tell me I was insane for doing.

Being president of the student body, however, I loved. I totally got the bug for collaborating with others to make government work and solving problems, albeit at that very small scale. In my state of the university address, I quoted Bobby Kennedy, which was maybe a little grand for the moment at hand.

"Some men see things as they are and say, 'why?' I dream things that never were and say, 'why not?'"

The torch had been passed.

Oof. Looking back now, I cringe. It was just the most extra, in every possible way. I rack my brain for how any single person could read that with a straight face. But there's no question that I took the job seriously. I chose not to run for reelection so I could spend my first semester of my junior year in Washington, interning on Capitol Hill. We had to interview for the position, and the only rule was that you couldn't work for your own congressman or senator. You had to earn it—not be given the slot. That was the theory behind the rules established by my political science professor, Richard Fenno. He was a well-known leader in the field and became a mentor to me and inspired me to go down this path that I remain on to this day.

I earned a spot in the office of Senator Carl Levin, who represented Michigan for nearly four decades. His office was on the fourth floor of the Russell Building and was ornate and beautiful and across the hall from Pat Moynihan's office, which made me a little starstruck when I'd see him in the hall. When I wasn't in the back sorting mail in the mailroom, my desk was literally right in the main entry to his office, so everyone would flow through right in front of me. I knew I was an invisible young kid answering phones, but to me, my position meant that I got a front-row seat to everything. I soaked in every last drop of action and learned faces and names and the way these people talked to each other and about the issues. I quickly figured out who cared about what, which staffers knew how to pull the levers, who got to brief the senator. I was working tirelessly, but it hardly even felt like work. It was action packed. It was busy. It was a million different things. It felt to me like I was at the white-hot center of everything.

Even though I was the absolute lowest person on the rungs of that building, I felt like I had the ball.

I would ask every staffer I met to give me something to do—a letter to send, a memo to write. I am sure that I bugged everyone, but I just wanted in on the game. I knew I was where I belonged and that I would end up back there after I graduated. I went back to Rochester to finish the rest of my junior and senior years. I was the student marshal at graduation, which meant I got to give a speech on stage to my classmates. It was a cold, blustery May day, not atypical for upstate New York, and I went from the ceremony back to my dorm room, packed up all of my stuff in my soft-top red Jeep Wrangler, and drove down to DC. I roomed with two of my college buddies in a house by American University. I got a job back in Senator Levin's office. I was still answering phones, but even with that, I just wanted to be the best at it. And this time, I was getting paid. Not a lot, but it was a real job. I wanted to answer more calls than anyone. I wanted to do the most right by the people who were calling their senator's office for help.

When a constituent called, I would answer. Instead of just

passing the note off to the staffer who was in charge of whatever problem they were calling about, I would carry the note down myself and say, "Hey, I just talked to this woman from Detroit and she had this problem. Can I see how you would work on this and fix it?" And then I would call that constituent back myself to let them know it was done.

I loved that feeling. It kept me going. Not that I was in charge in any way. I was the opposite of that. I was the most junior person there and I looked like I was about twelve years old. My suits were cheap and there's no chance they fit well. Regrettably, I was in a suspenders phase for some reason. I had no inclination at that time that I would ever consider running for office myself. That kid had no idea what would come later. I just felt that whatever my position was, I wanted to be the best at it. I wanted to be a leader in it. I wanted to get better at it. I knew that would propel me forward to whatever was next.

Pretty soon, it did. I was first promoted to legislative correspondent, which meant that I handled writing back to constituent mail, and then to legislative assistant, wherein I would be writing memos, doing research, and even briefing Senator Levin on some issues. Early on, I was asked to write a memo about a bill that was coming up for a vote on a matter of a woman's right to choose. Now, we knew where the senator stood on this. He was never going to waver on his support for that right. But this was my first big memo, and I wanted to get it right. I studied how other staffers wrote their memos. I spent hours on formatting it and I knew that at the end it looked perfect.

When I finished, the legislative director invited me to brief Senator Levin on what I'd written. I went into his beautiful, impressive office, where I found him behind his desk, reading glasses on the end of his nose, thumbing through my memo. I figured he would just say a quick thank-you, hear me make a few of my key points, and then go about his busy day.

He proceeded to ask me what felt like a million questions. Question after question after question. I had absolutely not anticipated this. In my head, I kept thinking, Senator, you are going to vote yes for protecting a woman's right to choose. Why are you even spending the time asking questions? It made no sense to me then, but now, and throughout my career on the side of the desk where Senator Levin stood, it is a moment in my early career that I think about a lot.

What Senator Levin showed me is that you need to be prepared for every possible question, every possible scenario, and you should always think through things from all angles, even when you believe you know where you will land on something. It is the fundamental underpinning of being a great leader. If you don't ask the right questions and listen to the answers, you can't make the right decisions.

*   *   *

A few weeks after I moved to DC, I got a call from Lori. She was coming down to DC for a job interview. Would I mind if she stayed with me? I agreed, despite the fact that I was still licking my wounds from the love letter humiliation years earlier. I knew there was a greater good.

She came down the night before her interview, and we stayed up irresponsibly late talking. I loved her. I'd always loved her. The feeling that we had that night, of being able to talk about anything and laugh together and feel so comfortable—that's what I wanted. We hadn't missed a beat. I wasn't going to let it go and screw it up this time.

I was thrilled when she got the job and moved to Washington. She moved in with a friend in an apartment in Adams Morgan, when that neighborhood was not quite what it is today. Her moving boxes weren't even unpacked when it became clear that it was not as safe as either of us would have wanted it to be. To no surprise, her mom promptly called me. Lori needed out of there. Would it be okay if she temporarily stayed with me and my friends? So we packed all of her stuff back into the boxes and she came to stay with us until she got an apartment in DuPont Circle with a new friend, Liz.

We got back together. Almost immediately. There was just one hitch. I was kind of dating someone else at the time. I knew nothing could start again with Lori until I ended that. I needed to sort that out. Quickly. I wanted to be honest; that was only fair to everyone. I didn't want to waste her time and I didn't want to risk giving Lori time to change her mind. So I told this other woman the truth—that Lori had come back into my life, and that she was the one, and that I knew I was going to be with her forever.

Within six weeks, we were engaged.

Now, we had no married friends. Few of our friends were even in serious relationships. I don't think either of us had even been to a wedding before our own. We were twenty-three years old. We had little money. We were still living with roommates, both working insane hours. But she was my best friend and it felt right. The stability in our relationship was all I had ever wanted growing up, and the reality was better than the theory of it I'd built up in my mind all those years.

I knew that I would propose in Israel, the place where we took our first trip in high school. My brother Adam happened to be studying there over the fall of 1995, so I had a reason to get her there without her suspecting anything. I knew that I wanted to buy her a diamond, but I had essentially no way to afford one. Someone told me that I could get a good price for one in the diamond market in Jerusalem. So once we arrived in the city, I went down there and chose the prettiest ring that I could actually pay for—a simple gold band with a small round diamond at the center, the ring she still wears today. One day, I always tell her, I will buy her the biggest, most beautiful ring she's ever seen. Every time she responds that she is not interested in anything other than what she has.

I called her parents from Israel to tell them my plans and to ask for her hand in marriage. They gave me their blessing.

A couple of days before I was going to propose, we joined Adam's class trip to Petra, in Jordan. It is a miraculous place. You access the famous archaeological site that dates back to 300 BCE through a narrow canyon, after which you are greeted by elaborately carved tombs and temples that were chiseled into pink sandstone cliffs, covered by stucco and painted in a sea of bright colors. It's known as the "Rose City," but truthfully, it has the feeling of belonging to another world. If you've seen *Indiana Jones and the Last Crusade*, you'll know where we were.

There I was, walking through all of this majesty, with her ring taped within my shorts pocket and anxiety clawing at my insides. I was terrified the entire trip that I would lose it. But I had a plan. This would be special. And I was finally going to get the girl.

Once we got back to Jerusalem the next day, my plan was to take Lori to a nice dinner in the charming neighborhood Yemin Moshe, known for the Montefiore Windmill. It's an iconic landmark in the city, built in 1857 on a slope opposite the western city walls as a flour mill with the hopes that the neighborhood could make its own flour to support itself and create jobs within the Jewish community. It remained unused but upright through the wars and stands above the city as a symbol. We had been there a few times together in high school, so as important as this monument is to the city, it was special to us, too.

We were staying in an apartment that didn't have reliable hot water, so when I told Lori she'd better shower after days of hiking through the sandy deserts of Jordan and change before heading to dinner, she said that she'd skip the cold shower and be fine to go to dinner as she was. I knew what was to come. I knew we were (hopefully!) getting engaged, and I assumed that she would have wanted to clean up for that moment.

I pushed her enough to completely confuse and annoy her, so by the time we did turn up for dinner, the night was not exactly starting off on the best foot. I was a wreck the whole meal, nervous and sweating and wanting to just blurt out the big question after every bite. Finally, dinner ended and we walked about a hundred yards to the windmill. I pulled out the ring, got down on one knee, and asked her to marry me. As I looked up at her to hear her response, the heavens opened. It started to rain. Sheets and sheets—I mean buckets—of rain came down. I don't even think she said yes before we both started sprinting down the street to find cover, laughing and crying and grabbing each other's hands.

"*Yes!*" she cried as we made it to the King David Hotel. We settled in, got some tea, and called her parents and mine. We were engaged!

We kept the celebrations going once we returned home. I knew that I wanted Valentine's Day to be particularly special that year. It was our last such holiday as technically single people, our first being engaged. I wanted to go all out. I surprised her with dinner at the Old Ebbitt Grill and tickets to see a performance of *Les Misérables* around the corner at the National Theater in DC.

During intermission, I went to the restroom. Standing at the wall of urinals I overheard a conversation that two guys were having. They were talking about what to do for their wives for Valentine's Day tomorrow. I returned to my seat, thinking these two guys were going to be in trouble for missing Valentine's Day, and shared the story with Lori. She looked at me, smiled, and I realized it was me who got it wrong, not those two dudes. I did the whole thing a day early.

I've never managed to live this down. To this day, we celebrate the holiday on February 13. We call it V-Day Observed, a testament to us doing it our own way, and making the best of whatever comes.

Our wedding was on May 25, 1997, at Lavender Hall in Bucks County, Pennsylvania. We invited about 150 people to our dream outdoor wedding. And, just as it has for nearly every other big moment in our lives, it poured rain. So we moved all 150 people inside the hall, which was absolutely too small for a wedding that size. It was hot. It was packed. But it was perfect. It was officiated by a whole crew of rabbis—the rabbi from my synagogue growing up and the rabbi from the one Lori went to, and the rabbi from our high school. The ceremony was infused with religion and tradition, our shared faith and history and all the blessings and hope for the future.

אני לדודי ודודי לי

I am my beloved, and my beloved is mine.

I broke the glass under the chuppah—the Jewish wedding canopy meant to symbolize the new home a couple will create together, open on all sides, so that they might welcome in their family and friends and G-d's presence.

I don't know what meaning can be drawn from the fact that I nearly broke my foot in the act.

We were such babies that none of our friends had been part of any weddings before in a real way. So when my college buddy Adam Keats was nice enough to buy us a special bag to put around the glass so we would be able to keep these sacred pieces of glass, he didn't know that (or maybe he did and he was messing with me) typically the groom stomps down on a lightbulb or something light and easy to break. Instead, he filled this beautiful little bag with a full-on heavy wine goblet, with a circular base that jammed right into the arch of my foot as I gamely stamped down in my moment of joy.

By the time I took my rented tux shoes off at the end of the night, after hours of dancing, I barely recognized my own foot, it was so bruised. And that's to say nothing of what happened when Lori and I got to our room the next day in St. Thomas on our honeymoon—in a little condo that was right on the beach and just feet from the ocean. I was so overcome by the view that I raced right over to take it all in, without realizing that I was barreling toward a very clean, clear glass wall. My head slammed into it cartoon style, with such force that I feared my skull and ego might never recover. Lori laughed hysterically once she was certain I hadn't blacked out.

I could have taken these as omens. But I didn't care. Not even for a second. And clearly, if anything, they pointed to the fact that we were just so content to be married that it didn't matter if I was hobbled and maybe mildly concussed. We were young and together and really happy. Our new life was beginning.

*   *   *

I was working my way up on the Hill. I was swamped, but I decided that I wanted to go to law school. I didn't know yet exactly what I wanted to do in politics, but I knew that that degree could only help, and I was genuinely fascinated and intrigued by the law. My hours were punishing and Lori and I were newlyweds, neither of which left me much time to study for the LSATs.

Unsurprisingly, I did terribly. I stunk at standardized testing. But I applied to night school at Georgetown, George Washington, American University, and Temple, hoping that my work in Congress might give me a little bit of a boost. I got rejected from AU, GW, and Temple. By some miracle, Georgetown accepted me.

I was baffled. My scores were awful. The other schools flat-out denied me. Georgetown was by far the highest ranked of the bunch. It made no sense to me. So I called the admissions office and got the dean on the phone. I asked him why he accepted me.

"Usually, these are the kinds of calls I get from people who get rejected," he said. "I've never had someone who got in call and question my decision." He told me that my grades were strong and that my work experience was impressive. It was clear that I was driven to do this and had a reason for being. I told him that I planned to be in public service for a long time, that I didn't know if I would earn enough to be a meaningful alumnus donor. But if I ever achieved anything and could do anything to help repay the university for giving me this shot, I promised to pay it forward. I made good on this years later. I've gone back to campus to speak at events, recounting this story, in fact.

Lori went to get her master's at GW at night, while I went to law school at night at Georgetown. For night students, law school is spread out over four years, instead of the typical three. In my first few years, I would wake up early to read for class before working all day on the Hill. I'd then go to class from 6 until 9 o'clock at night, when I would come home, read some more, prepare for whatever was ahead the next day for my actual job, and then go to bed and do the whole thing all over again.

Lori and I carved out time for each other and ourselves. We lived in a small two-story condo near the National Cathedral in a community called McLean Gardens. We'd go for hikes on the weekends with our golden retriever, Baxter. We decorated our apartment. I tried to fix things when needed. There is a fair amount of lore within my family about my handyman skills. On one side of the argument, I can mostly take anything on. On the other side, Lori often cites the time that the skylight in our DC apartment started leaking. The apartment was a loft, and the ceilings soared, and I decided that I was going to do something about it. In the midst of all the things I was balancing at home and in school, I was also going to fix our leaky skylight. Of course I was going to fix it—that's what a husband is supposed to do. Well, as Lori tells it, she walked into the apartment to see me on the twenty-foot extension ladder I had borrowed from our neighbor, and immediately started to scream, "You need to get down. Slowly. You need to come down right now." Because she noticed that I had set up the ladder upside down.

Had I not noticed that the steps were round? That safety feature that is built in to make sure that you know when a ladder is right side up or upside down? I guess I missed that part.

She will then bring up the fact that in that same apartment, I had tried to fix another leak, this time the kitchen sink faucet. She gave me an eye roll at my plan, left the apartment, and went about her day. When she returned a few hours later, she could hear me on the phone with her dad, John, an MIT-educated engineer and incredibly handy man, muttering quietly into the phone, "I don't want to fix it anymore. I just want to figure out how to put it all back together. It's fine if it leaks."

Her storytelling on this disputed subject usually rounds out with one final detail. Our place was just down the block from a local hardware store called Hechinger. As it's now clear, I took on enough of these projects and needed enough rescuing from those projects that the guys down there had come to know me. One afternoon I brought Lori along with me as I stopped to pick something up. I introduced Lori to my friend working behind the register as I checked out. "This is my wife," I said.

The guy held out his hand to shake Lori's, looked my way, and bowed his head. "I am sorry," he said. They both had a good laugh.

* * *

In January 1999, I moved over to Congressman Joe Hoeffel's office. He had just been elected from Montgomery County, where I grew up, and so it was an easy fit. He gave me a shot. I started off as his legislative director, and within a few months, he made me his chief of staff. I was told at the time I was the youngest chief of staff on the Hill, and usually, the youngest guy in the room.

By 2001, Lori was pregnant. Sophia, our first child, our only daughter, was born on October 20, one month and nine days after the horrific attacks on September 11.

I was at the Capitol on the morning of 9/11 in my office, where we later learned one of the hijacked planes was possibly headed. Lori was working in Arlington, at a building not too far from the Pentagon, where a hijacked plane did hit. All of the bridges in and out of DC were immediately closed down, so Lori, who was also evacuated, wound up at the home of a friend of a friend of one of her colleagues across the bridge in Virginia. She was nearly nine months pregnant. The cell phone lines were jammed, and we had no way of being in touch for hours.

The woman who had taken Lori in was a mom, and it happened to be her kid's birthday the following day. As they all sat there glued to the television watching the news unfold, they tried to lighten the mood by talking about their families and the little things they did to mark their happier moments. The mom explained her annual birthday tradition: She would sneak into her kids' rooms while they were sleeping and decorate with balloons and streamers. When they woke up in the morning there was a surprise celebration waiting for them as they opened their eyes.

Eventually, the cell towers started working and the bridges opened. After that day, the group that had gathered together never saw each other again. They never exchanged information. Lori doesn't even remember this woman's name. But this tradition is something that we continue in our family to this day. For all four of our kids' birthdays, we do what she taught Lori that day— celebrating the gift of life and making those birthdays special. We think about her, and the shelter and the light she provided in the midst of such horror, on every one of those days each year.

Lori made it home to our place in DC that evening, as chaotic and on edge as the country was. We tried to ground ourselves in as much normalcy as we could. Even with all of the darkness around us, we tried to find the light. And there was enough to focus on.

Like everyone else, we took it all seriously, and as a soon-to-be dad, I was extra on guard and bought the extra emergency water and other stuff we were told we needed to keep us safe. Lori and I did what we were told. She went to Harris Teeter, filled her cart with as much water as she could fit, and, as she should have done, left it in the trunk of our car for me to bring inside.

We lived in a third-floor walk-up. Just the idea of lugging all those jugs from our parking spot about a hundred yards away to our apartment exhausted me. So they lingered in our car for far too long. I was working on the Hill, which meant that every day I'd go through security first to park my car, then go to my office. It was always a precise and tight process, but at the time it was understandably especially extensive. So I'd drive in every morning, and the National Guard, who were all over the Hill at that point, would open my trunk to make sure the car was clear and I was safe to go in. I remember one guy just laughing at me as I explained to him that I hadn't gotten around to carrying them inside our house just yet. He took to calling me "water boy" each day when I'd pull up.

Of course, when I eventually did get around to bringing them all inside—the heroic pillar of strength that I am—I shoved all that water into a closet underneath the stairwell that housed our coats that we never really used, where they lived until we eventually moved out. As we were emptying the closet, we pulled out thirty empty jugs that once were quite full atop a totally warped floor. It turns out that the plastic from the water bottles that had been cooking in the trunk of the car for weeks on end was causing them to expand and contract over and over again.

So that when I did eventually get them inside, the plastic was so weakened that they had tiny pin holes in them that slowly let water out over time. Those gallons leaked straight through the floorboards. Years later, I told my friend, former Pennsylvania Governor and our nation's first Homeland Security Secretary, Tom Ridge, how I was prepared and what I'd done with that water. We still laugh about it.

We were classic first-time parents, crossing every T and dotting every I, doing all the things everyone tells you that you absolutely have to do in order to bring a life into the world and keep that little person alive—none of which I think you actually have to do, by the way. But what do you know before you know it? So we went to a birthing class, like lots of other new parents do. I've never paid more attention than I did in those hours. I was laser focused, committing to memory every breath Lori might need to employ, every way I could possibly be helpful or take control in a situation in which we had very little control, in a moment where I could not possibly be all that helpful. We got to the point where they asked us to get down on the ground. I sat with my legs out and Lori sat in between my legs, resting back onto my chest, so we could practice how I could support her. And while I was focused like a laser beam on the directions from the teacher while holding Lori, she started shaking. I panicked, of course. Was she okay? Was she going into labor? Was I going to have to put all of this into practice, like, immediately?

I jolted forward to make sure she was okay, only to see her hysterically laughing and trying to hold it in at the same time. She could not keep it together. She was unstoppably giggling at the absurdity of it all. "What is wrong with you?" I whispered, looking around the room at all the other serious, focused couples. "Get yourself together."

"I can't," she said. And so I caught her giggle. We were both in hysterics. We could not help it. It was just so ridiculous. We had to let the pressure out of the balloon.

We were promptly sent straight out of the class. We grabbed lunch at Pizzeria Paradiso, promised ourselves we would get ourselves together, and returned to class after lunch. We walked back in, locked eyes with the teacher, and lost control again. We couldn't stop laughing. She sent us on our way and asked us not to return. Birthing class dropouts. Delinquents of the highest degree.

About a month later, on the day Lori went into labor, I found out that someone had sent anthrax to one of the offices on our floor on the Hill. We were at the hospital, and I was in a full-on panic that I had somehow been contaminated. I was intent on not upsetting Lori. That moment was not exactly a time for Dad to be bringing the drama. So I secretly flagged down our doctor and asked him exactly just how risky was it for me to be there and how I was going to negotiate the fact that I couldn't quite tell Lori what was happening. I absolutely did not want to miss this birth, but I also did not want to infect everyone with a poisonous substance that I really did not know much about.

Anthrax poisoning wasn't contagious, the doctor explained, so he told me to go back in the room with Lori and put me on a proactive dose of Cipro.

Sophia arrived early in the morning. For that moment, our troubled world righted itself, our hearts filled. I had loved Lori for more than a decade at that point, but the depths of that love just quadrupled. I thought I'd known faith, but now I knew G-d. And that little girl—she was the key to everything. I would do whatever I could to protect her, to love her, to do right, to be good and make good. As soon as I held baby Sophia, I was prepared to give up my life for her. We were a family. A unit. I wanted to do a lot of things in this world, and I have, but that was the only thing I knew I had to get right. Unconditional, absolute love for my family.

*   *   *

After eight years, I knew that it was time to leave DC. Lori graduated from GW and earned her Masters Degree. I had graduated from law school and risen enough in the ranks for there to only be three options if I wanted to continue to grow: I could either be a chief of staff for a more senior member of Congress, practice law, or go to K Street and lobby. Those were the conventional paths, and ones I totally respect. They just happened to not speak to me. On the personal side, it was nagging me that for as much as we were enjoying our time in DC, it just didn't feel like home, like where we wanted to raise a family, coach basketball, and plant roots. We did love it there and had great friends. But it wasn't home.

I had been walking down the hallway to the floor of the House one morning, ready to brief as I'd been for the last many years, when I just knew in my bones that I didn't want to do this anymore. I pulled my BlackBerry off the holster on my hip—yes, I wore my BlackBerry on a holster on my hip, as I am sure Gary Cooper would have done, along with the many pleats on my pants—and called Lori. "I think it's time that we move back home."

*   *   *

It was pretty much a given that we would move near where we grew up. All of our parents were around, which would be wonderful for Sophia and as our family continued to grow. In the spring of 2003, I got a job at Ballard Spahr, a large law firm in Philadelphia, and we bought a house that we could afford, that we knew we would fix up over time, in a great neighborhood. It's where our family still lives today. When we woke up in the house after the first night we slept there, Sophia, who was two at the time, looked out her window from her crib at our yard in the back. She pointed to the swing set the previous owners had left. "Park!" she exclaimed. Even this little urban toddler couldn't contemplate that this nature belonged to us. It was ours. It was home.

I was putting in my hours at Ballard. The people were great. Everyone treated me with such kindness. I was making good money. But I didn't care for the track—really, treadmill—of being a corporate lawyer. It was just not feeding me in a way that made me feel good about my place in the world.

There was one day in particular I realized this wasn't going to be my calling. I'd heard a commotion outside my small office. I wandered out. A bunch of lawyers had gathered to celebrate a big win for an insurance company. It was a victory. That was their job. They'd done good by their clients. That just wasn't the side I wanted to be on. That wasn't my victory.

So I was listening for the call when it came.

Not long after, in the summer of 2003, I got involved politically in our new hometown of Abington—next to the town I grew up in. Joe Hoeffel announced soon thereafter that he was vacating his congressional seat where I now lived to run for the US Senate. This set off a cascade of political events. Some people even encouraged me to run for my old boss's seat. Instead, I launched a run in September of that year for the state House of Representatives against a longtime, popular, moderate incumbent Republican named Ellen Bard. Republicans like Ellen was are now mostly Democrats in today's politics. Soon after I announced my run against her, she decided to run for Congress for the open seat instead. That should have been good, except the new opponent—a former US congressman with 99 percent name ID in Abington and high approval ratings on his home turf who ironically lost his congressional seat four years earlier to Hoeffel—was not any easier.

Still, this race felt like fate. And it felt like the right job for me. It was in an area I'd known all my life, with people I'd lived alongside for my whole childhood, and now, I was a local husband and dad who'd cut his teeth on DC politics. I cared about the issues in our area, and I knew that I could represent these people well.

There were some hitches, however. The district was Republican. Overwhelmingly so—at about 60 percent. The guy I would be running against, Jon Fox, a veteran Republican, had already served as state representative, county commissioner, and congressman. His party saw the race as a lock for him. And they should have, with his résumé and the makeup of the district. I was thirty years old and had just moved back to the district about a minute earlier. Yes, people knew my parents—especially my dad, as the local doctor—and I guess it impressed some people that I had worked my way up in DC. But I was, for all intents and purposes, a complete unknown.

But I believed that with hard work I could win. I just needed to figure out my way in. I started showing up to local Democratic events. There was one meeting for the Abington Rockledge Democratic Committee—known as the ARDC—in particular where I pulled a few regulars aside and told them that I wanted to run for the seat.

I knew that I would need to raise money if I wanted to be taken seriously and to start building name recognition. So I went back to DC to hold a fund-raiser at one of the bars close to the House side of Capitol Hill. I invited all the staffers I'd worked with on the Hill, friends from law school, anyone I'd ever come across in DC who had seen how I worked. Most of them thought that I was crazy to leave the Hill in the first place. Now they thought I was absolutely nuts, not only to run for office, but to run for state rep in what looked like an unwinnable district.

I understood why they thought that, but I was going to take the ball and see what I could do with it because it felt right.

I walked away from that night with around twenty-six thousand dollars, which felt like an enormous sum of money to raise at that point in the race. As locked as this race seemed to be for Fox and the Republicans, the Montgomery County Democratic Committee was pushing every election cycle to grow its Democratic delegation in Harrisburg. They were willing to put money behind this race, and there were two other Democrats vying for it. Rather than slugging through a messy primary, the ARDC decided they would run a screening committee to decide whom to nominate. We all agreed we would endorse and come together behind whoever they decided would be the best candidate based on a series of interviews they'd conduct with each of us. My two opponents had been members of the ARDC for years. Everyone knew them, rightly, because they paid their dues. Each served our community as township commissioners. They were good guys who were more than qualified.

I went through the interviews, and the committee voted for me. They saw how hard I was working, that I had a vision and the desire to do, and thought that I would be the right candidate for that moment, despite how green I was. As we agreed to, the other two candidates dropped out and supported me. To this day, I am grateful to Wayne Luker and Michael O'Connor for honoring that commitment and giving me a shot. It was my first real big political break. I was on top of the world. For a moment, at least, until I caught the eyes of two women sitting in the front row of the ARDC meeting room.

Their names were Marge Sexton and Pat Conroy, and they'd been local Democratic fixtures forever. "You can't win," they said, cutting me down to size.

With everything stacked against me, I tried to get rolling. No one really wanted to work for what folks assumed would be a losing campaign. Well, except for my sister, Rebecca, who had as little experience on campaigns as I did. She was there and willing, so she was in charge and ran my campaign. We would turn up at local political events in Abington and the Republicans in charge wouldn't let me speak or even acknowledge me. I came home to Lori at night, after being trounced all day, complaining that I couldn't even get in front of people. If they wouldn't let me speak, how the hell was anyone ever going to even know me, let alone vote for me?

"It sounds like you're going to need to figure out a way to talk to them," she said. "And for them to talk to you."

I probably left the room in a huff. She doesn't understand, I thought. A comment I would mumble under my breath a million times in the years to come, only to learn a few minutes, months, or years later that of course she understood far better than I did and she was generally almost always right. It was her way of challenging me to find my place, trust my gut, and gather my strength. The next day, I pulled out a pair of comfortable shoes and began walking from house to house and just started knocking. I was figuring out a way to meet my neighbors.

*   *   *

I knocked on eighteen thousand doors over the next few months. First on my own with a clipboard. Then with my first dedicated volunteer, Jean Corrigan. Then a few more. What else was I going to do, honestly? I just gutted it out. Much like I had when I was in law school while working on the Hill, I spent the early hours with Sophia before heading downtown to work at Ballard. By four o'clock, I would train back to our district and start knocking on doors until it was dark out or well into dinnertime, when people would be annoyed to see someone on their front step. I'd get home around eight, which meant I would get Soph time, if I was lucky and we could stretch her bedtime. After she was asleep, I would write notes to everyone I'd met that day, thanking them for their time and for telling me what was on their minds. It was exhausting. Law school at night prepared us for this grind. Through it all, Rebecca was building a team and organizing a great campaign. We didn't really know what we didn't know, but even though the numbers didn't show it, it felt like something was working.

No one was telling me to do this. I was just hungry. I really wanted this. I believed in what I was doing. Rebecca was there to prop me up. All of those things propelled me to keep going.

To get a sense of just how low budget and shoestring our first campaign was, we didn't have money for a professional photo shoot for my headshot like other candidates would. So we had one of my brother's friends (who had studied journalism and is now actually a writer at the *New York Times*, I am sure due in large part to this great and storied work experience) come over and take photos. It was kind of a cold day, the lighting was poor, and my face was deep red from the chill in the air. But I had an American flag hanging up on our porch, which is still hanging in the same place in our home in Abington, and we took a photo of me on the porch with the flag behind me. That became the picture we used on my campaign cards. So if I knocked on a door and someone wasn't home, I would write a note across the card and my bright red face saying that I was sorry to miss them but that I would follow up. And I did.

Initially, as I knocked on those first hundred or so doors, I tried to tell people my views on education, health care, and issues that kept their streets clean and businesses thriving.

I quickly learned that no one really wanted to hear me go on and on. They didn't want to be talked at. They wanted to be listened to and they wanted to be heard.

So I changed my approach very quickly. I would knock and say, "Hey, I'm Josh Shapiro. I'm running to be your state representative. I'm going to work hard for you. What's on your mind? What would you like to see change? How can I help?"

More often than I would have imagined, the first words out of people's mouths were, "Hey, wait, your dad is our pediatrician!" It's the part of this story my dad likes most. I could have been embarrassed by this, already the youngest guy in the race by far, but it was my ID badge, and a reason to keep pushing forward. He had taken care of families in this area for so many years. He listened to them. He trusted them to know what they needed. That's who I wanted to be for them, too.

A lot of the time, folks would tell me about the problems they were facing getting good medical care. Or not enough teachers in their kids' schools. Every story stuck with me. I knew that I wanted to actually solve these problems. I'd come home totally beat but completely energized by the people I met and the stories they shared. I'd race through the door to relay all of this to Lori, and she'd look at me, deadpan, and say, "I can't believe people even open the door for you when you knock. I would never do that."

After Labor Day 2004, we took a poll. I was down 65–21. Brutal. Even though my numbers were still below freezing, I started to feel like I was gaining some momentum. I could just feel it. I was able to raise some money. I had no network, but I called every single person I could get on the phone asking for money. If you were willing to give the campaign fifty dollars, I would all but break into a song and dance.

Eventually, the powers that be started to get involved. Governor Ed Rendell came out offering me his support, which was a big deal at the time. He did a fund-raiser that brought in a bunch of donations, which we desperately needed. He believed in me. The Montgomery County Democratic Committee saw the movement, and, eager to gain more seats in the legislature and inch toward a majority in the Capitol, started spending in the district. It became one of the most expensive legislative races in the state. About half of the money we ultimately raised came in the last two months of the race. The wind was at our backs. I was running an obsessively positive campaign and closing the gap. Then my opponent went negative on me. He opened the door. And it backfired, because of all those doors people opened for me when I knocked on them. They didn't like the kid who showed up at their house unannounced listening to their concerns being attacked.

There was a lot of attention on the district—not only for my race, but also because it was a key area for John Kerry, who was running against President George W. Bush that year. Governor Rendell called me and told me that he wanted to host a rally in Abington, and that he was going to bring a campaign bus with a bunch of celebrities. It was a huge deal at the time, both because he was as eager as he was to support me and because he was going to bring that kind of heat to our home base.

We managed to get the local Teamsters union to let us borrow a flatbed truck, which we decorated in the parking lot behind our tiny campaign office, which shared a parking lot with the video rental store. Rendell and his crew rolled up in their much more official campaign bus to see us waiting there. We must have looked like such rookies. One by one, stars got off the bus and climbed up onto our flatbed—first Rendell, followed by other Pennsylvania politicians. Then came Danny Glover. When I saw Christie Brinkley emerge, I did a double take. She reached for my hand for help climbing up.

As everyone got on board, we handed out Shapiro for State Rep stickers. Christie asked me to put one on her chest. I looked over at Lori, who was holding Sophia and just barely keeping in her laughter. We both would have thought we'd imagined the whole thing if not for the photos of her standing behind me at the podium wearing that sticker as I gave a speech to the crowd we'd gathered.

I felt good. I was hitting my stride. The jump shots were falling no matter where I was on the court. I was confident. But I had never been in this game before, on this court. So it was hard to have a good feel for this game in the final stretch. A few days later, on the night of the election, Lori and I were at our house, waiting on the returns that Rebecca was tabulating in the campaign office about five minutes away. Back then poll workers had to call in their results to the office. We didn't hear anything until my sister turned up at our door—it was before text messages and Twitter. She banged on the front door, ran in, jumped into my arms, and started screaming, *"You won! You won!"* She hadn't wanted to tell me over the phone.

We ended up winning by more than nine points.

We had no real experience on a campaign. There was no secret sauce. I believed in myself and hard work. My sister did an incredible job and like always, had my back. We had a very small but extremely mighty team, including a young guy named Matt Vahey, who now serves a township commissioner in Abington. We were all willing to do the work. We showed up, knocked on those doors, made the calls. I listened. They listened. We all listened. And listened some more. Now, the real work began.

It's worth noting that Marge Sexton and Pat Conroy, the two local Democratic fixtures who were skeptical of my candidacy at that first ARDC meeting when I wanted to run for office, ended up being two of my most enthusiastic volunteers and stood with me when I was sworn in as the new state representative for the 153rd Legislative District.

★   ★   ★

Once I was sworn in, I immersed myself in the issues. I stayed close to Governor Rendell, who would call to check in or invite me over to the Governor's Residence late at night after a session to go over provisions of a bill he thought I should lead on. It was super flattering to have the Governor as a mentor. He was instrumental in my learning how to navigate Harrisburg and find my lanes early on.

The hardest part of the job for me wasn't the schedule or learning the ropes or finding my way on the issues. It was being away from my family. In April 2005, about four months after I was sworn into the Pennsylvania state House, we had Jonah, our first son. We always knew that we wanted to have a big family if we were so fortunate. It's one of the fundamental things we agreed on early in our marriage. I was going to be where my family was, plain and simple. Which would mean that I would have had to drive back and forth between Abington and Harrisburg. I'd sit in a car for as many hours as it took as many days as I needed to if it meant I'd get ten minutes with my kids or with Lori, but I couldn't stand the idea that this time away and time commuting meant that I was taking more than I was giving. I skipped the lobbyist dinners and much of the Harrisburg nightlife and instead was constantly racing home trying to be the best version of a dad.

I was really only there with them half of the time. And when I was home, I was splitting that time between my family and the people I represented. In the seven years I served as state representative, I held more than a hundred town hall meetings for people in my district. Usually about forty or fifty people would show up. I'd give a report on what we had done and what we were hoping to accomplish in the near future, and then I would open the floor up for questions. I wouldn't go home until I answered every one. To this day, I think I am comfortable being as accessible and honest with people on a public stage as I am because of all the time I spent listening to and answering to these folks in these town halls. I loved those town halls and the interactions.

All of this made me look like a little bit of an upstart to the old guard. I understood that and took their ribbing in stride. When I would get up to speak on the House floor, the veteran guys would call out, "Freshmen aren't supposed to talk!" In private, though, almost all of them were supportive and well-meaning.

One senior member from Philadelphia in particular stopped me as I was walking up the aisle to leave the floor. He'd been there forever, a former dockworker at the Philadelphia port, a committee chair, and now one of the guys who warmed the back row with the best of the old-timers. The place you'd go for some wisdom and ball busting.

"Hey, Shapiro," Rep. Bill Keller called. "You can't get there from here."

"Where's there?" I asked.

"Wherever you're going, you can't get there from here."

* * *

At first I was offended by that. I fought to get "here." Here is where I wanted to be. But I sort of knew what he meant. And I knew it was from a good place. I had only been in the job for a few months at this time, but he knew that I knew I wasn't going to stay there forever. I loved the work. I respected those guys. I had no plans to leave anytime soon. I didn't know where "there" was, though.

By the time my first reelection rolled around in 2006, I had been working nonstop. I held all those town halls to show my work and stay connected to the listening part of the job. I had raised a few hundred thousand dollars for my reelection campaign. Still, they ran a guy named Lou Guerra against me, and he seemed like a real, formidable candidate. Plus, the district was starting to change, but it was still more Republican than Democrat at this point, so I knew that my victory was not a given, even as an incumbent. I took nothing for granted and I campaigned like a total maniac. Whenever his campaign would file its funding reports that would detail donations made to the campaign,

I would reach out to the person or business who donated to his campaign to introduce myself, listen to what they had to say, and explain how I would like to represent them and help make their lives a little bit better. I door-knocked the hell out of every house around where he lived and where his family went to church. I didn't take my seat for granted and I wasn't going to leave a single vote on the table. I earned 76 percent of the vote.

The same was true two years later, in 2008, though by then, the district had started to move into more Democratic territory. I was registering voters and the Obama election was a seismic shift. The Republicans had struggled to find a candidate to run against me in time for the filing deadline. I had heard that they were getting the word out to rally behind a write-in candidate, which made sense. But I, of course, had gotten rather used to the idea of running unopposed. So I wrote each Republican I knew and helped along the way explaining that I would appreciate if when they went to vote in the upcoming GOP primary they could write in my name on the ballot. I know you're a Republican, I wrote, but I will continue to work for you, just as I worked for the Democrats.

It worked. I won the Republican primary on a write-in defeating the candidate the GOP Committee was supporting. I also won the Democratic primary, which essentially meant that I was running against myself.

*   *   *

My first reelection was especially meaningful. My colleagues and I had just come off a tough session in the state House. In the minority, Democrats had struggled to pass a big environmental bill, and we were aware of the fact that as long as Republicans were in the majority, we weren't going to get much of anything we cared about through. And then there was the fact that many of them had given themselves a nice, fat pay raise—34 percent higher in some cases—in a vote that took place at two o'clock in the morning and just before they went on a two-month-long recess. (For the record, I voted against the pay raise and didn't accept the new income.) There were other public scandals brewing at the same time. All of this fired up voters, leading to an inordinate number of incumbents retiring and nearly 50 percent of the state House turning over in the 2006 cycle.

As a result, Democrats took the majority in 2007, but with a 102–101 margin. We were keenly aware of the thin margin we were operating within.

Bill DeWeese, the Democratic floor leader and our Speaker-designate, whom I'd grown quite fond of, called me just before New Year's to tell me that he was hearing that at least two Democrats were going to defect from the floor vote for speaker, for which 102 votes are required—which would cost us the majority and him the speakership. Our hard-won majority control was going to go back to Republican Speaker John Perzel, who many people believed—correctly—was corrupt. I was worked up, knowing what that would do to our agenda.

At this point, we were visiting my sister Rebecca's family with Sophia and Jonah. We had gone out to dinner at the Chart House in Los Angeles, and I was telling Lori how frustrated I was by possible defections. I'd been complaining about this to her for days already.

"Instead of complaining about it," Lori said, "Do something about it. I'm sure you can figure something out." Sure, I thought. Easy. I was barely a second-term lawmaker with little clout. I had worked hard with others to make sure that we won the majority, but there was no way I was going to "figure something out" like she said I would. There was no time, and I had no formal role or power to affect the process. We were set to vote on the speaker-ship in two days, right after the New Year. "What am I supposed to do?" I asked her. Nobody else seemed to have a plan.

We flew home on New Year's Eve Day, and that night, I hopped in the car to pick up Chinese food before Lori and I settled in to watch the ball drop.

I stopped at a light at an intersection at the center of town and had a flashback to being at that same spot three years earlier. At the time, I was campaigning for my first election, holding up my lawn signs as oncoming traffic whirred by and trying des-perately to get my name out there to voters who'd never heard of me. One kind driver gave me a thumbs-up as he raced by, and I noticed that he had a state legislator license plate. The guy who'd given me the thumbs-up was Denny O'Brien, a longtime Republican rep. In today's politics, he'd probably be a Demo-crat, but not back then. There was a lane for folks like that back then. We knew each other as colleagues, but we weren't bud-dies or anything. I knew that he didn't get along with Perzel, which could have been reason enough for him to at least hear me out.

Driving through that same intersection gave me a crazy idea. What if we Democrats nominated a moderate Republican like O'Brien to be Speaker? Maybe we could pick up some other moderate Republican votes to absorb the Democrats we thought were defecting. A bipartisan, consensus Speaker. Something never done before in Pennsylvania.

I had no authority to make that call. I'd asked no one's per-mission. I hadn't even uttered the idea out loud before I called

O'Brien on New Year's Eve. "Denny, it's Josh Shapiro. You wanna be Speaker?" I asked.

"Sure," he said in an instant. "How are you possibly going to do that?" he asked.

"Well," I said. "I don't know yet. But hang with me."

I hung up and dialed DeWeese.

"Happy New Year, Scout," he answered, using the nickname he'd given me. I wasn't sure if at the time he thought of me as a Boy Scout or it was a reference to the Old Testament, in which Joshua was the main scout that Moses sent into Canaan. He had a gift for the English language and he knew his Bible. It could have been either. I told him that we had O'Brien.

"He's going to vote for me as Speaker?" he asked. I told him that no, he was actually going to *be* our Speaker and DeWeese would be Majority Leader and in effect preserve the majority we worked so hard to attain. I then made a call to Dave Steil, another moderate Republican from Bucks County in the mold of Bard, O'Brien, and so many other GOP leaders in that day. I explained the concept. It was hardly a plan yet. Steil, a truly honorable man, disliked the way Perzel ran the House and hated that the institution we both loved felt beyond repair and in need of dramatic reform.

The next morning, on New Year's Day, I asked the caucus leaders to meet me at the Marriott in West Conshohocken, right off the Pennsylvania Turnpike, to work through the specifics and make a plan. We got Governor Rendell on speakerphone. O'Brien agreed to become Speaker of the Democratic majority as long as he could remain a Republican. DeWeese would be the majority leader, and Democrats would hang on to our ability to set and pass the agenda.

As I drove to Harrisburg for the New Year and new session, I got a call from O'Brien, who seemed to have cold feet. We agreed to meet at the Governor's Residence before he made his final decision at the Capitol in a few hours.

Once we were all together, in the basement rec room at the Residence, we talked him down. Some tried to woo him with the promise of a better pension and a bigger salary. I knew that wouldn't work; that didn't motivate Denny. He was in it for the right reasons—to help others. But he still had this lingering doubt. He didn't know if he could go against his own party like that, and without warning, at the last second.

Rendell's chief of staff, Steve Crawford, knew that O'Brien had long been a champion of children with autism. At so many legislative sessions, he'd held up photos of these kids, whose causes he supported. Steve told Denny that as Speaker in this unique construct, he could take those three-by-five pics of kids with autism and turn them into eight-by-ten glossies and pass something meaningful to finally help them.

With that, Denny was in, and we all headed over to the Capitol. The vote was in an hour.

Lori and the kids had driven in for the day, and they were waiting for me when I got to the House floor. Usually guests are seated along the edge of the chamber. Lori was in my seat with both Sophia and Jonah on her lap. "Do you have a plan?" she whispered to me. All of this was still a secret, to both sides of the aisle, apart from our small group—the Democratic leaders, Ed Rendell, and me—working behind the scenes.

"I think so," I muttered.

"But is it going to work?" she asked. I didn't answer.

Truthfully, I had no idea. Would Steil be able to bring along other Republicans? Would more than two Democrats defect? Would the rest of the rank-and-file House Democrats like me vote for a Republican for Speaker?

You can't get there from here, I thought. I might not be able to stay here if this doesn't work.

When the opening legislative session started a few moments later, after all the ceremonial stuff was over and the process to elect a Speaker began, Republican Perzel knew he had the two Democratic defectors in his pocket. He had 103 votes—he needed 102. DeWeese began with the nominations for speakership. Everyone in the room had expected to hear DeWeese's own name along with Perzel's. When he came out with O'Brien, there was an audible gasp in the chamber. I watched as the reality dawned on Perzel's face. He leapt out of his seat and ran straight to the back of the House floor, where O'Brien was sitting with the Republican old guard. These two had been rivals for years, and from neighboring districts in Northeast Philly, so the tensions had been long simmering. Now all of it boiled over. Neither of them would make eye contact with the other, but I could see Perzel side-eye O'Brien and through gritted teeth, say, "Do. Not. Accept. The. Nomination." Over and over he repeated it.

O'Brien ignored him. The Democrats in the chamber were going nuts, too. The powerful appropriations chairman, a friend named Dwight Evans, was running up and down the aisles telling Democratic members to trust us and to vote for O'Brien. How could we vote for a Republican, members asked. It was chaos. But it worked. All but two Democrats—the two that we had known were going to defect from the beginning—voted for O'Brien. We picked up a few Republican votes, too, including Steil.

I ran over to O'Brien and was asked by DeWeese to formally escort him up to the front of the chamber and take his place on the Speaker's rostrum. I took the gavel, gave it a bang, and into the microphone, said, "Members of the House, distinguished guests, I present to you the Speaker of the House, Denny O'Brien."

*   *   *

After the session adjourned, I walked with him to the Speaker's office, a room I'd never been in before. Perzel was the previous occupant and certainly never invited me over. We were all stunned, unable to fully take in what we'd just pushed through. It worked, I thought. It really freaking worked.

We all patted each other on the back before parting ways. Ironically, one of the first people I saw as I left the room was Perzel. I knew him to be a political bully who worked hard to defeat me over the years, but he appreciated good politics when he saw it, and he had certainly just had a front-row seat.

"Nice job, kid," he said as he walked down the hallway. That would be the last time we spoke until about a decade later when we bumped into each other on a crosswalk on Broad Street in Philadelphia just after he returned to the city from serving nearly two years in state prison on corruption charges.

*   *   *

The new Speaker's first act was to create a bipartisan commission to reform the state House. He had wanted me to chair it, but I thought it would be better for Steil and me to cochair it together as a bipartisan task force. Steil agreed.

It's always made sense to me to work with people across the aisle. Certainly, in Pennsylvania, a place with an independent streak that has sent Republicans and Democrats to the state House and the White House. Nothing can get done if you don't work with people in both parties. I'm never going to compromise my principles, but I am not going to be a purist, either.

We passed a bunch of meaningful reform measures through

that commission, and the work fueled me. Real politics, real progress.

After about five years in the House, I felt like it was time. I knew that I didn't want to move up the ranks in leadership. I was feeling more and more pulled away from home and my kids because I was in Harrisburg so much, the kids were getting bigger, and our family was growing. Max was born in 2009 and Lori was pregnant with our fourth child in 2010. Even when I was home, there were events to go to every night in our district. I was a little burned out, and all of the work that used to fill me up was instead draining me. I questioned for the first time whether I was feeling this way because I didn't want to work in public service or if I just didn't want to work as state representative anymore.

My gut told me it was the latter. Tired of the back and forth and the waiting around for process and caucus politics, I wanted to be an executive. I wanted to lead and call the shots and get shit done for my community in a different way.

You can't get there from here. I was beginning to understand.

I decided that I should run for county commissioner in Montgomery County, my home county of eight hundred thousand. It was an executive role, like being a mayor of a big city, really. I could be home with Lori and the kids, with less travel and way fewer nights away and missing bedtime. The only problem was that since the Civil War era, no Democrat won the top spot. The notion of Republicans losing control of the Board was almost unthinkable.

But, of course, I was undeterred. I took it on.

Beyond the history, the race was complicated by a number of other factors. The county commissioner's race is an unusual dynamic, in which four people run for three spots. In the near century and a half before my election, two Republicans had always won, leaving any Democrat who won the third seat in a powerless minority. I felt pretty confident that I would be one of the three candidates who'd win, but I didn't want to be the only Democrat elected. I'd have no power if that were the case. So I wanted to run alongside another candidate, arms linked, as the first Democratic duo to do so in about 150 years.

If that wasn't uphill enough, I was also in the position of potentially unseating Hoeffel, my former boss who'd given me a shot as a kid on the Hill. He was the minority commissioner at the time, after losing races for the US Senate and Governor, and he was struggling politically. He was wrapped up in a local scandal over a Republican violating some sunshine laws with colluding outside of a public meeting. He hadn't done anything untoward and had not been accused of anything illegal, but the Republican he was working with had, and just the association with the scandal unfairly marred him. He had no campaign money in the bank, and the party leadership had lost faith in him. Local Democrats wanted me to run against him, because they knew that I had the ability to win. It was deeply uncomfortable and tricky for me, and I tried to handle it as delicately as I could. I met with him a number of times to hash it out. As tense as it was between us in those moments, I was fully honest with him about my intentions and where I saw the race. He vacillated between telling me that I was trying to screw him over—which I was not—and asking me to run alongside him, as the Democrat who would link arms. I knew that I couldn't win with him, and I knew that it wasn't the right thing for the party or the county, even if we could somehow eke out the victory. I told him that I would never run against him, if he decided that he was to seek reelection, but that I would not run with him. If he really wanted to go forward with it, I would have stayed in the state House. But if we wanted to have a chance to win as Democrats, he would have to step down and endorse a new ticket.

Hoeffel ultimately decided not to run again, which I am certain left a bad taste in his mouth. I'd hear about him talking to the press or to people behind my back about how he thought I lacked loyalty, that I was someone who needed to be watched. It felt terrible, and of course, I never intended to hurt him in any way and I would never have run against him. I wanted the Democrats to have a shot, and I knew that I could get it done.

Once he stepped aside, I linked arms with Leslie Richards, a fellow Democrat. We beat the odds and broke the century and a half long Republican spell over our county in 2011. Looking back, that was the election that started the mass political shift in the Philadelphia suburbs. The GOP committee once singled out by Ronald Reagan as one of the three best-led Republican counties in America collapsed, and within just a few years all of the other counties shifted Democrat as well.

*   *   *

We hired a great new team and quickly got to work. There was a lot to do. We inherited a bunch of messes. First, my predecessors had been mired in those corruption allegations. (This somehow has become a running theme throughout my career: I've had to come in and clean up after getting elected a couple of times.) The county's financial situation, as the result of 140 years of straight Republican control with little oversight or pushback, was an absolute disaster. There was a huge hole in the budget. The literal facade of the county office building was crumbling and falling to the street. It was a physical manifestation of all the problems in a most basic way.

The good news was that with Richards, our agenda would be able to sail through. For the first time, I was able to hire and run a real executive team. About four thousand people worked for the county. They knew I cared about them and the work, so the office developed a real esprit de corps. Our senior staff, including Ray McGarry, Uri Monson, Lee Soltysiak, and Frank Custer, and led by our outstanding COO, Lauren Lambrugo, was talented and motivated. I loved working with them.

As I'd learned on the Hill, I knew that this team would be absolutely crucial. At every step of the way, it was always important to surround myself with people who had unique skills that I did not have, who grew up differently and brought different experiences and viewpoints to our decision-making process, and who had the strength and courage and intestinal fortitude and courage of conviction, who had the confidence to speak their minds because they knew I was open to it. If you want to be a good executive, you have to hear different voices around the table, and have people around you who can say no. It's a process that we've relied on and fine-tuned as our teams have gotten bigger, something I credit Dana with for helping me build those subsequent teams. We had a lot to get done, and this was my first executive role, so I had knowledge and experience gaps to fill.

If there was a job for them to do, I was going to do it alongside them. A problem to solve, we'd be in the trenches together. In my first few weeks on the job, it looked like we were about to get walloped with a major snowstorm. Typically, the public works department dealt with preparing the roads and plowing, but as Chairman of the Board of Commissioners, all of this fell under my purview, so I wanted my hands in it. I had about a million questions about who did what and when. I just know that the emergency preparedness folks were, like, "Why does this guy care about all these little things?" But if I was ultimately responsible for this, I had to try to understand it all. I wanted them to know I was in it with them and had their backs.

I also wanted the residents in the county to know that we were on top of things, working with a talented team to keep them safe and letting them know what was going on. I held weather briefings, which I am sure sounded goofy, but communicating and showing that there is someone doing the job has always been super important to me.

When the storm did come, and it was as bad as they predicted, I shoveled out of my house to make sure that I could get down to Norristown, our county seat. I wanted to be there with the emergency response crews. I wanted to see how it was done. Not to check up on them, but to learn from them.

I don't think they expected that they'd have the county commissioner riding the snowplows with them on the road, but I hopped right on as they went over county roads. This was the job, and I wanted to know and see and touch it all.

I was serious about the emergency preparedness in the county. I spent a lot of time at the Emergency Operations Center, which was not something a lot of commissioners before me had done. I knew the team appreciated the fact that I wanted to get to know them and understand their work and show up, so they made me an emergency hard hat with "Commissioner" emblazoned on it.

I loved it. I was so excited to bring it home and show it to the kids, who I knew would get as big a kick out of it as I did. Jonah took a look at it and asked why I had it, what was it for? I told him that if there's an emergency, Dad needs that protective hat. I was beaming.

"If there's a real emergency," Lori said, "it's not your dad in a hat that's keeping us safe." Humbled, as ever. Right, of course. It's good to know that there's no chance I'll ever not be grounded.

Much as I was enjoying getting right into the work with the team, the first thing we needed to fix was the $10 million budget deficit. I knew that I wasn't going to make any meaningful change if we just tinkered with the existing budget. We needed to start from scratch.

I proposed we do this by implementing zero-based budgeting. I'd always been intrigued by this idea. Rather than relying on previous budgets, we would go through every single expense and justify us either keeping it or cutting it as if it was the first time we were funding anything. We had every department come to us with their objectives or goals, along with a cost associated with what it would take to achieve those things.

Truthfully, if it sounds similar to the intended purpose of the Department of Government Efficiency, that's because it's pretty similar.

The lesson is that execution matters as much as implementation, and the way we implemented zero-based budgeting was with the intent of reducing waste and increasing efficiency without creating chaos.

With every dollar, we asked the same question: Is this supporting the core function of government? If we couldn't answer this affirmatively, then we cut their funding to zero. If it was worthwhile, we'd fund it.

In year one, we cut the budget overall, but as a result of our approach, we simultaneously found ways to invest more in the areas that needed it most. Our budget was balanced by the end of the first year. By year four, overall spending decreased and output increased. Our credit rating went up. It was real progress and important for the county. We didn't need to blow up the entire system and cause disasters in order to get there. There was no wrecking ball. It just required critical thinking and the willingness to do hard things. We carefully and methodically made significant changes with real, tangible impacts. Ultimately, the county wound up much better off. You can create progress without chaos.

The commissioner job was expansive for me. I learned so much about managing a big staff and running the operations of a government. I was challenged so often in my ability to make quick decisions. Every day, I saw how much I relied on the extremely qualified, reliable people around me so I could juggle all of this and quickly come to conclusions, and then be able to execute them.

When Leslie and I were initially elected, we didn't anticipate that we could have the buy-in from the third county commissioner elected. Bruce Castor was a top Republican dog in the district, and we had slugged it out in the campaign in the four-person race for the majority. We hadn't crossed paths much before this, but I reached out to Bruce right after the election to talk. He invited me to lunch at The Aviation Club, a small dining club, adjacent to a small airstrip in Blue Bell.

"Look," I said. "The campaign is over. I want to work with you. You have a lot to offer and I think we can both accomplish what we want to if we work together." He agreed. We decided that we would divvy up areas based on what we were interested in. If there was something that he wanted to focus on, I would empower him in that space and take his advice on it. When it came time to pass an ordinance, if he felt strongly about something, I would try to meet him where he was as long as I could understand his reasoning.

We were both on the same page and ended up hitting it off.

Over the course of four years, there were fewer than a handful of times when we didn't vote the same way. The rest of the time, every vote was cast 3–0. That allowed us to really make headway. Not only with the budget, but also on a number of practical matters, like expanding our trail network and fixing more bridges than ever before. We increased human services in the county and fully funded the public defender office for the first time in a long time. The three of us—Leslie, Bruce, and I—were a political odd throuple, but it worked.

In hindsight, I credit these years with my success early on as Governor. I had learned so much about what it takes to be an executive, how to build a great team, and to work with people across the aisle that I felt like I had a giant running head start on the role.

For as smoothly and fruitfully as we worked together, our alliance was met with resistance from our parties. Castor caught a lot of fire from Republicans for working with me the way we did. I got a bunch of guff from Democrats, too. I will tell you: it was worth every bit of nagging we got, because we worked seamlessly and effectively and got a lot done.

I think back to this time, especially in our current political moment, in which there are not many examples of politicians reaching across the aisle to find common ground and commonsense solutions. All I can say is for this all to work we can't be fearful of the political backlash and must practice real leadership.

Now, none of this has changed for me, even though the climate definitely has.

I still reach out to Republicans and try to find ways to work with them. Modern-day politics discourages this, but I won't give up on it. It's what I've learned over the years—if you truly want to serve the people who elect you, fix what's broken, and make a positive impact, you have to build coalitions even with people you disagree with.

If I have to face some blowback in order to get those things done, so be it. Folks know, though, I won't back down from a fight when someone is trying to mess with people I'm sworn to protect. I won't blow with the political winds. I do what I think is right, and I'm not afraid to stand up for it, to anyone.

That's always been my philosophy, even back to the county commissioner job.

After four years of us working together this way, Castor left the job to run for district attorney. Leslie had left a year earlier to join Governor Wolf's Cabinet and I brought on Val Arkoosh to take her spot on the Board. I won reelection and continued to chug forward for the county, though over those years I had been approached several times to cast a wider net. The first time was in 2012, when Congresswoman Allyson Schwartz left her seat to run for Governor. I think everyone was sure that I was going to run to fill her vacant spot. It was a safely Democratic seat. I was popular in her district. It was as much of a political layup as you could get.

I also happened to be in a really nice rhythm, in the county and at home. By then, Max was a toddler, and we just had our fourth, Reuben, in January 2011. I knew that with four young kids and a job I loved, the move to DC would be tough.

Some aspects of that appealed to me. I thought back to my time as a staffer, walking in the majesty of those buildings on the Hill. A bunch of my former colleagues were still working there, so I had an easy cohort that I could jump back into.

Lori, for all that she was juggling, didn't discourage me from doing it, but she challenged me to make sure that I actually, really did want it. Buy a train ticket, go there, sleep over, walk around the Hill, she suggested to me. Come back home, and if you think that life is for you, then you should run.

I did just that. I saw a bunch of my old buddies, who had become really senior-level staffers by that point. I went to a few of the old places I'd go to for lunch or to unwind after a long day. I listened to my real friends, who knew me and grew up in this business with me, like Scott Mulhauser and Mike Merola, discourage me from a run. A buddy who's a national political reporter even told me on a walk around the Capitol how broken the system was and how much better my gig seemed back in Montgomery County. By the time the sun went down, my feet were tired, but my hotel was only a short walk. I looked at my watch. If I left now, I thought, I could make the last train home.

I didn't even want to spend one night in Washington, let alone do this every single day.

The thing that kept playing in my head was that I didn't want to let go of my ability as an executive to get stuff done. Going back to the legislature and that whole process, of being in a caucus, engaging in the performative arts on a daily basis, felt like a move in the wrong direction for me and heading further away from the growing family that I was working so hard to be present for. I have plenty of respect for what those members of congress do; it just wasn't for me.

A couple of years later, I weighed a similar decision when Senator Harry Reid, the Democratic leader at the time, together with Senator Chuck Schumer, was looking for someone to run against Senator Pat Toomey in 2015.

Home was chaotic and crazy in a good way. With kids activities and my work in the county, I had more than enough to sink into. I felt real purpose in it, in all of it, and the longer

I stayed in that job, the more I got to see our work bear fruit. At the same time, I was aware that I wasn't going to stay in the role forever. I knew I had more room to grow and different paths I wanted to take. Being a US senator is a big deal, and to be someone the leadership thought could win that race and do the job felt like an honor. Over the course of six weeks, I spent time with Schumer, Reid, and my good friend Senator Bob Casey and visited DC again. They did some polling and Senator Schumer made some real financial commitments to my campaign, if I wanted to run.

I was really torn.

As part of the process, I talked to Senator Chris Coons, who had done a version of my county commissioner job in Delaware before he became a senator. He told me I get more done every day as a county commissioner than I would as a US senator. When I asked him why he joined the Senate, he explained that while it might take ten years in the Senate to accomplish the task, it would have a more far-reaching impact. A number of others lamented but verified that pace when I asked them about what Senator Coons had told me. To this day, I appreciate their candor.

I had a hard time getting that timeframe out of my head. For as mighty as it is to be a senator, to me it felt more purposeful to be in charge, making the calls. To make the progress and see, day in and day out, the work playing out around you. I didn't want to miss those days with my kids and my wife, either. I waffled still. I had one last night before I had to give Senator Schumer an answer.

"Why do you want to do that job, to be a senator?" Lori asked that night, when we finally got to talk about the day before bed after the exhausting ritual of doing bedtime for four children.

In a huff (a common theme you'll note), I responded with something like, "It's a US senator."

She continued. "Because this isn't the only job or path you could take from here. What is it about *this job* that's appealing to you?"

I sat there quietly. Honestly, I couldn't come up with a compelling enough reason for why I would want to do that work every day. There's honor in the work our senators do, it just wasn't for me.

"Actually," I said. "I think I want to run for Attorney General."

That was not the traditional path for someone with my political background, and I was not the most obvious candidate, given that I had never been a prosecutor before. In that way, it was a much bigger stretch than the Senate, which at that point made much more logical sense and seemed to be a more direct path.

"Then why would you do anything other than that?" Lori asked.

I called Senators Reid and Schumer the next morning to pass. Reid wasn't surprised—he and his right hand, David Krone, knew my heart wasn't in it.

"Oh," Schumer responded. "You're one of those people who likes doing stuff. You like the action. Go do your stuff, then." He wished me the best.

*   *   *

It took a fair amount of soul searching to make sure that this was the right next step. The flip side was that I didn't fit the typical Attorney General mold, and the job itself was going to be really different from anything I had ever done. I was out of my comfort zone, for sure, but I needed to just make a decision and run with it. I was hand-wringing, something I am not known to do. I searched and prayed for clarity. Something I am known to do.

As I was mulling the next move in the fall of 2015, a Democrat named Stephen Zappala Jr. from the Pittsburgh area jumped into the race. He was a longtime District Attorney of Allegheny County. His dad, Stephen Zappala Sr., had been a Justice on Pennsylvania's Supreme Court. He couldn't have had more name recognition in our state's judicial system. His family was all politically active. It's hard to think of someone who had more legal experience or was more establishment than this guy.

He was everything I was not. His strengths were my weaknesses. His path *was* the path you took if you wanted to become Attorney General one day. And he knew that he wanted the job, so all through the fall and holidays of 2015, he was locking in support and raising money.

I won reelection as county commissioner that November, with more votes than anyone had ever gotten for that seat. By December, I assembled a campaign team led by Dana and Joe Radosevich and told them that I was ready to move. Let's do it, I said. We made calls in a small, moldy, damp room in Norristown near the county courthouse from the minute I decided until early Christmas Eve night. We were full on.

Despite my victories in Montgomery County and my travels around the state supporting other Democrats and getting to know more folks, I was a hard sell to the local powers that be. They questioned if I was the right person to do that job, given that it was perceived to be centered around courtroom experience and, well, I had none. They weren't wrong. That was hard to argue with. But my vision for the job was different from what it currently was and always had been. Of course, the courtroom aspect of it would be a vital function, and I trusted that I would learn those ropes and handle that piece of it just fine.

The way I saw it, the office could be much broader than just being a traditional prosecutor. If it were me in that seat, I would make it all about being a crusader for the people and a protector of the rights of all Pennsylvanians.

It could be the office that helped all of these folks and protected their interests. In that way, it would be the next logical step. Yes, the scale would be greater and the processes different, but I'd get to combine all the reasons why I went into public service with my executive experience and ability to lead a team.

People said I was crazy for talking about the job in those terms. That just wasn't what prosecutors did, they told me. Voters wanted a guy who they were sure would be a legal eagle for the cases at hand—a guy like Steve Zappala.

I wasn't convinced that they were right. I knew that we were onto something with this broader vision for the job. We did some polling to test my theory. We asked whether it was good or bad if Josh Shapiro had never prosecuted a case in court. We also asked whether it was good or bad that Zappala had spent twenty years prosecuting cases. The answers confirmed my suspicions: Voters didn't seem to care that I hadn't spent time in a courtroom or that my primary opponent had. What they actually wanted was someone to stand up for their rights and protect them.

That led me into the primary feeling even more confident and determined to broaden the possibilities of the office. To center it more around the people. I knew that I would outwork him, and I knew that the central argument he was going to use against me was not compelling to voters. Even still, that primary fight just sucked, as it always does when you are fighting with your own people and party. It was hard fought and got pretty nasty.

Predictably, they came at me hard on my lack of prosecutorial experience. I punched back, too. I wanted to win, and I found an edge in the fight.

"You should ask Obama to endorse you," Lori said one night as I lamented how icky it all felt.

President Obama and I had known each other for a decade, and we had always kept in touch. I mean, as in touch as you can stay with the President. We'd get invited to the White House to celebrate the holidays and for parties, and I had a warm relationship with his body guy and trusted personal aide, Reggie Love. Even still, I thought Lori's suggestion was nuts. He was the President of the United States. The country was in the midst of a national campaign with the soul of the nation on the line. This wasn't even a Senate or House race. It was a primary race, for Attorney General. You think he'd give a damn about that?

"In all these years, you've never asked him for anything and he's always told you to reach out if you ever need anything. What does it hurt to just ask?"

I brushed her off as I am known to do. I am also known to listen intently to what she says, process it, and then usually find my way back to where she started with scant info, no formal training in politics or governing, but with the keenest eye and the sharpest sense I know.

And, yet, the more I thought about it, the more I knew that Lori was right, as usual. My political team told us in no uncertain terms just how delusional we were, that there was no chance he would ever do it. Saul Shorr, my dear friend and brilliant political adviser for two decades, told me there was "less than a 1 percent chance" he'd do it. Saul can see around corners, and I so trust his judgment. But I decided I'd lose nothing by asking—and I kinda wanted to prove Saul wrong. I called Love and asked him for his advice on how to best go about making the ask. He told me that he suspected the President would be willing to consider it.

*   *   *

I first met Obama in the fall of 2006, in the final days before my state House reelection. Ed Rendell was Governor, and there were big races on the line that cycle in both the House and the Senate. By that point, it was looking like Bob Casey would unseat Senator Rick Santorum. Rendell wanted to whip up the base in that final stretch with a string of big, buzzy, packed, star-studded rallies. He knew I had my act together and that I was an ally, so he called me on a Friday night. "I've got a bus going throughout southeastern Pennsylvania tomorrow. I want you there," he said. "You can either do the morning rally with Al Gore, or in the evening with Barack Obama." I thought back to that first rally behind my campaign office.

Now, at that point, I'd known who Obama was, but didn't *know* him. I was definitely intrigued by the way he communicated and the way people seemed drawn to him, but Gore was the big name.

I was a first-term state rep, and Rendell was giving me basically hours' notice to pack a rally in the suburbs of Philadelphia. I needed as much time as possible to get a crowd together, so I told him I'd do the event Saturday evening with Obama. That would give me a few more hours to build the thing.

I immediately started scurrying around trying to get our community, friends, and neighbors to agree to come on Saturday. We booked the Keswick Theater, which holds about thirteen hundred people. I told the folks there that there was no way we were going to fill it, so they should just put up some curtains around half of the theater so I didn't look like an idiot in front of Rendell. I spent the rest of the day making calls and begging as many people as I could to show up at the last minute. We leafletted and got the word out as best we could.

When I got to the venue an hour or so before the event, there was a line around the block. The people working at the Keswick had long since taken down the curtains.

They were turning people away from the front of the Tudor Revival–style venue. We filled the place! Well, the promise of Obama filled the place.

Rendell, Casey, Nancy Pelosi, and my buddy Patrick Murphy, who was running for Congress, were there, along with a host of others. Lori had Sophia and a very tiny baby Jonah backstage. It was electric in there and I was trying to soak it all in when Rendell came up to me and looked me in the eye. "Start the show," he said.

Well, I said to myself. This crowd doesn't want to hear from me. They want to hear from everyone else here. But I wasn't going to say no to Rendell. This was my turf. I guess the Governor wants me to emcee, so let's go.

One by one, I introduced the heavy hitters, who took the stage and gave remarks. The crowd was amped. It was clear that they were all there to hear the young senator from Illinois, and their excitement was contagious. I wanted to hear him just as much as they did.

The only problem was Obama wasn't on stage yet. He was outside talking to his advisers. I didn't know at the time that when he eventually did make it into the building, he had gotten waylaid backstage chatting with Lori and our young kids. All

I knew was that I was getting whispers from Rendell to keep stretching and stretching as we all waited for the main event.

Eventually, he made it out there, and I was relieved of my vamping duties. I stood just behind his left shoulder and watched in awe of how he commanded the stage and spoke to everyone we'd miraculously managed to gather there at the last minute. He had few notes. He connected with all the faces in the crowd. His voice rose and fell. They were rapt. So was I.

Once the event ended, I walked him out of the theater. "Look," I said. "I don't know if you're going to run for President, but if you do, I am all in. I want to be the first."

When he did announce his presidential campaign, Rendell and the old guard Democrats were lining up as many influential people in Pennsylvania as they could to get behind Hillary Clinton. I've always really, really liked Hillary. She is incredibly sharp. Very few people share her experience and wisdom. But I really believed in him, and I wanted him to be President. It was the first time in my life I felt that way about a candidate.

I was willing to use what very little political capital I had at that point, and I told Rendell immediately that I was going to support Obama.

At the time, I don't think Rendell really cared. I was still a baby politician. He had way bigger fish to worry about. He did make it clear that me stepping out of line with him and the old guard could cost me down the line, but that didn't sway me. He also told me that Hillary was going to win, and I needed to carefully consider being on the wrong side of her. I wasn't against Hillary in any way. I was for Obama. I was already comfortable marching to my own beat. I was respectful of my political elders, but I was always going to be true to who I was and whom I wanted to support. Even if it looked like that person was an underdog, even if all of the other big politicians in the Commonwealth were behind her. In hindsight, it was a savvy move, but at the time, it was probably a little risky. But I was really struck by Obama. I thought he was kind of a once-in-a-lifetime political figure and that I could learn something from him. Rendell was nice about it. He busted my chops enough, and then we moved on to working together as we always had.

Initially, Obama didn't spend a lot of time in Pennsylvania because of the primary schedule. It didn't look like he was going to win anything, until of course there was lightning in a bottle and he won Iowa. The pendulum started to swing, and I helped his campaign organize the new support and endorsements as they started coming in. He didn't have a huge infrastructure in the Commonwealth yet, so I would be there every time the campaign came to Pennsylvania. I got to spend a fair amount of time with him on the trail. I got to see how calmly he reacted to all of the hype and attention and expectations. How warmly he treated his family and his team.

By the spring of 2008, he had ripped off a bunch of wins and had a delegate lead. There was a long gap in between when the primaries in March were held and when voters would head to the polls in Pennsylvania at the end of April. It was in this lull that the videos and writings from Pastor Jeremiah Wright surfaced. Wright, Obama's longtime pastor in Chicago whose church he attended for twenty years and who officiated his wedding, had made a series of comments that were unpatriotic, anti-Israel, and antisemitic. The backlash hit hard, and Obama responded quickly and clearly in a way that I respected. At the same time, Wright's comments were outrageous. I was upset by them, and I knew many people in the Jewish community in Pennsylvania and around the country and world were, too. Rightfully so.

Obama's team invited me to join them on what they called a whistle-stop tour across part of the state. It harkened back to the train trips of Abraham Lincoln and Harry Truman. It was like we were moving through history.

"You can't go," Lori said the night before. It was the start of Passover that night. "We have to be at my mom's. You need to be here." It wouldn't be a problem, I told her. I'd pop by 30th Street Station, where the train was departing, and give Obama a quick wave, though he likely wouldn't even see me in the scrum. Maybe I'd crowd into the caboose for a stop, and make my way back home to help move chairs and set up the house with plenty of time. Probably even before lunch.

I should have had an inkling when I got to the station and an aide brought me onto an adorned train car—that Truman himself had taken—with Senator Bob Casey and two of Obama's longtime friends and advisers, Valerie Jarrett and Eric Whitaker, that I would not, in fact, make it home before lunch. It wasn't until I saw Obama walk on and pull the train's whistle that I knew I was in trouble.

We went four stops, from Philadelphia to Harrisburg. Obama asked if I wanted to join him at his own Seder that night at his hotel in Harrisburg. I politely declined and explained I needed to be home with family. He totally understood. I made it back just in time for the start of the Seder.

During our train ride, we sat around a small dining table and talked in really personal terms in between stops. I mostly listened. He was staring down several weeks without a primary election and the coverage of his former pastor. He talked about the impact the race was having on his kids and at the same time the lift he got from meeting Americans in their communities. It seemed like he was grappling with the same issues I was working through—albeit on a much larger stage.

I listened to Obama explain the Wright situation. He said how connected he felt to the Jewish community and how important the community was to him. I didn't feel like it was fair to hold him accountable for something his pastor said, particularly if he was as quick and as clear in articulating what he did believe in and what he did stand for. I was struck by how pained he was by this. Not because of what it was going to do to his political chances—and at the time, it really was a *thing*. "I've worked so hard throughout my life and my career to have such a strong relationship with the Jewish community," I remember him saying to me. "In fact, I've been accused by some people in the Black community of being *too* close to the Jewish community; that's how much I care about my relationship." It struck me as very genuine. Hearing that made me want to double down and really support him and have his back.

I caught heat for this support within the Jewish community. I went to a bunch of different synagogues and community groups to debate the issue. Privately, I was fielding a bunch of calls from donors who were nervous about his support of Israel, but I felt comfortable defending his beliefs. I thought the attacks were unfair. I believed in his message, and I thought that he would make a better President.

I gathered a group of about three dozen prominent Jewish leaders at Rodeph Shalom, a synagogue in Philadelphia, to let them hear from the senator and ask questions about where he stood on Israel and Wright. I gave brief remarks at the beginning, letting them know that I believed in him, but that I wanted them to get the chance to see where he stood and

The burned-out rooms inside the Governor's Residence.

Dan Zampogna / Commonwealth Media Services.

The burned-out rooms inside the Governor's Residence.
Dan Zampogna / Commonwealth Media Services.

Meeting John Wardle, Chaplain of the Penn Township Fire Department, which responded to the attack on the Governor's Residence, while serving lunch to the firefighters who saved their lives that night. Chaplain Wardle gave Josh a letter signed by every member of the fire department with a prayer for his family written on the back. It was the same prayer Josh says over his children nightly.
Dan Zampogna / Commonwealth Media Services.

Early childhood photo of Josh.
Photo courtesy of the author.

Josh and his sister, Rebecca, at the US Naval Base where his dad, Steve, served as a medical officer. *Photo courtesy of the author.*

Special to The Inquirer / BARBARA JOHNSTON

Josh Shapiro of Akiba looks for a way to get the ball past defender Larry Bernstein of Wyncote.

Josh competing in his high school basketball championship game in 1991 (they won!). *Photo courtesy of the author.*

Lori and Josh in high school.
Photo courtesy of the author.

Lori and Josh on their wedding day in 1997.
Photo courtesy of the author.

Josh's sister and first Campaign Manager, Rebecca Steinberg, watching returns on Election Night, 2004, with her then-fiancé Jon Steinberg, now Josh's brother-in-law.
Photo courtesy of the author.

First interview as State Representative–Elect on election night, 2004.
Photo courtesy of the author.

Josh and his wife, Lori, walking into his Election HQ at the Glenside, PA, VFW after winning his first election for State Representative, 2004. *Photo courtesy of the author.*

Swearing-in on the floor of
the Pennsylvania House of
Representatives in 2008.
His son Jonah holds the bible.
Commonwealth Media Services.

First time meeting President Obama in 2006.
Photo courtesy of the author.

On the floor of the Pennsylvania House of Representatives.
Commonwealth Media Services.

Speaking in the rotunda in 2009.
Commonwealth Media Services.

At a rally with President Obama on the campaign trail in 2022.
Photo courtesy of Shapiro for Pennsylvania.

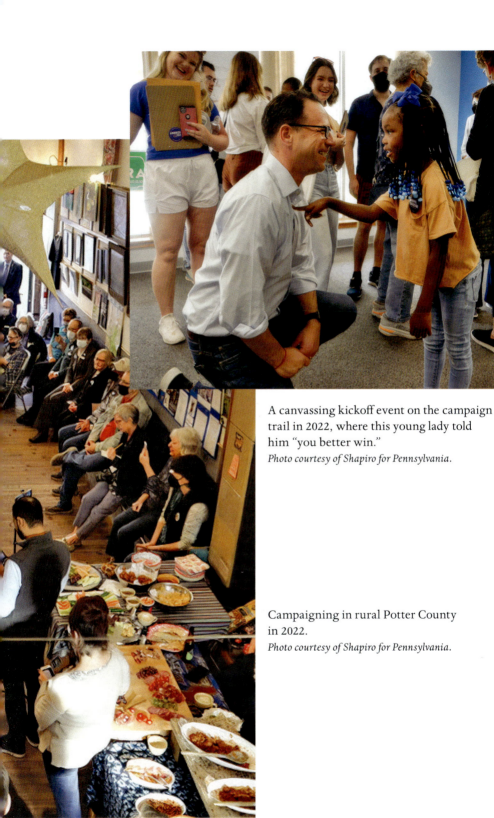

A canvassing kickoff event on the campaign trail in 2022, where this young lady told him "you better win."
Photo courtesy of Shapiro for Pennsylvania.

Campaigning in rural Potter County in 2022.
Photo courtesy of Shapiro for Pennsylvania.

A rally in Luzerne County on the campaign trail in 2022.
Photo courtesy of Shapiro for Pennsylvania.

Knocking doors in Montgomery County on the campaign trail in 2022.

Photo courtesy of Shapiro for Pennsylvania.

Josh and his family on election night eve, 2022.

Photo courtesy of the author.

Attorney General Shapiro rallying for legislative protections for victims of sexual abuse in 2018.

Commonwealth Media Services

With victims of abuse within the Catholic church.

Commonwealth Media Services.

Speaking at the DNC in 2024. *Photo courtesy of Shapiro for Pennsylvania.*

Speaking at the Ebenezer Baptist Church with Senator Warnock in 2024.
Photo courtesy of Shapiro for Pennsylvania.

Josh and his family at the Governor's Residence.
Photo courtesy of the author.

what he believed, in his own words. He spoke that night about repairing the relationship between the Jewish and African American communities, and how he wanted to be part of that necessary work.

*   *   *

We would see each other when Obama would come to Pennsylvania, and I kept up with Reggie, his body guy. In 2009, a few months into his first term, President Obama put together a small working group on health care reform, which ultimately led to some of the foundational ideas that became part of the Affordable Care Act. It was made up of about a dozen elected officials from across the country, and we met in the Roosevelt Room with the White House's health care policy leads to talk through broad strokes and what the priorities should be.

At the end of one session, Reggie grabbed me and said he wanted to show me around the West Wing. We wound through the narrow corridors and hallways. We poked our heads into all the little offices to say hi to folks settling into their new roles. We were hanging out in a nondescript office when I heard someone call my name from behind what I thought was a wall but turned out to be a door.

"Yo! Josh!" I heard. "Come on in here!"

It was President Obama, beckoning me from the Oval Office.

He gave me a hug and thanked me for the work I was doing. It was early on enough in his term that he hadn't redone the Oval yet, so much of President George W. Bush's decorations were still up. His photographer came in while we were catching up and snapped a few photos, one of which I've kept on my shelf ever since.

We took a photo like this together after my "Real Freedom" speech in North Philly at the end of my campaign running for Governor. John Fetterman, who was running for Senate, and President Biden were also speaking, all of us leading up to President Obama. It's not the least intimidating spot I've ever been in, I can say definitively. But I felt locked in on the speech. I had no notes. I knew I felt what I was saying. I knew it landed.

Once Obama finished his remarks, I went back out on the stage and Obama gave me a little bro hug. "Yo man," he said into my ear. "I was listening to your speech. It was damn good. There's something to that."

Holy shit, I thought. He listened to my speech? It's a moment I still carry with me. I keep that photo of our embrace in my office, too.

*   *   *

All of this is to say that I felt comfortable with and confident in my relationship with President Obama. Reggie told me to write an email asking for his endorsement, and he would make sure that it got to his desk.

And then I waited.

A week or two went by, and with the business of the campaign and work as usual in the commissioner's office, I'd pushed it aside in my mind. I was walking down Market Street in Philadelphia, where I was spending more and more of my time fundraising by speaking at one law office then the next, when I answered an unknown number. It was the White House political director, David Simas, calling. He had just come from a meeting with President Obama, he told me. He's going to endorse you. He'd put out a statement and we'd be able to use his voice in an ad. I called Lori immediately. She was right again. I also relished calling Saul and letting him know that the one percent chance hit.

We put up signs of us together all over Philadelphia. When I would drive through the neighborhoods and see them, I couldn't believe it was him and me together on that poster. It was an honor. I looked up to him so much and here he was, the President of the United States sticking his neck out there for me.

*   *   *

I won the primary for AG and went into the general feeling strong. I was ahead for most of the race. Democrats in general were confident that year. Hillary Clinton was on the trail, running on optimism in contrast to Trump's steady beats of fear-mongering. I started to notice bigger crowds showing up for Trump in areas that should have been competitive, and smaller and smaller crowds for Clinton rallies. In the summer of 2016, I visited Ag Progress Days in State College. An old Republican buddy of mine whom I served with in the state House pulled me aside and warned me that I shouldn't attack Trump as I made the case for my campaign in those places. They saw him as the clear winner and a transformational figure who could upend the traditional turnout models and projections. I heard that more and more as the days went on—confirming what I was seeing on the trail. The polls would tighten as the weeks wore on.

Now, my campaign really had nothing to do with Trump. I didn't talk about him or attack him in general. I was focused on the people and how I was going to protect their rights. I was naturally steering clear of the national issues, but the message from these Republicans stuck with me as an early red flag that my party was, in fact, in trouble.

I made it a point to visit and revisit communities that I'd never spent much time in, counties and districts and neighborhoods most Democrats often skip, knowing that they're never going to win there. That didn't matter to me. Maybe I would be able to pick up some of their votes if I went there. I'd welcome that. But that wasn't the only goal. I wanted these folks to know that even if they didn't vote for me, I was going to show up for them. I would fight for them just the same.

Many of the people I met in these places didn't agree with my political philosophy. They didn't share my same faith. We didn't grow up in the same kind of places or go to the same school or get the same degrees or understand the ins and outs of each other's jobs. But we understood what it felt like to be a parent. We were all watching our kids grow up in an era where, for the first time in our lives, we weren't sure if their futures were going to be as open to possibility and prosperity as ours were. I listened to them way more than I talked. Just like I learned while knocking on all those doors.

I found myself trying to be a sponge, to hear about their communities and learn what they needed. I wanted their votes, but I wanted more than anything to make their lives better, to help get the things done that they really wanted and needed.

What I learned in these communities really did help inform the kinds of promises I made on the trail. I vowed to take on the fentanyl crisis. I promised to create a labor protection division and an environmental rights division and to help fix inequities in the education system. I wanted health care to be better and more affordable and consumers to have faith that they wouldn't be scammed or jerked around by the big companies. I wanted to work closely with law enforcement to keep our streets safer.

This was uncharted territory for an AG in Pennsylvania, but it seemed to be catching on. A few weeks out from election day, our polling had me up a handful of points, above the numbers that Clinton was pulling. She was losing ground each day, it seemed.

On election night, I ended up being the top vote getter on the ballot, ahead of Clinton, who lost by about 44,000 votes, despite the fact that I was third on the ballot. Our Democratic nominee for Senate, just above me on the ballot, lost, too.

I made a point to be everywhere that year. I went to the suburbs. I went to the exurbs. I went to the rural parts of the state. I was up, down, left, right. Clinton's campaign had her mostly in Philadelphia and Pittsburgh and those surrounding areas. When we analyzed the numbers post election, we saw that in Philadelphia and its suburbs, Pittsburgh, and Allegheny County, Clinton and I basically both ran parallel—our numbers were virtually the same. It was everywhere else that I did better than her. (And, by the way, the same was true with Biden four years later.)

I had shown up. I listened. Voters felt that, and now all I wanted to do was deliver for them.

★   ★   ★

As Attorney General–elect, I set out my agenda with all of the promises I had made along the trail. I intended to make good, and I did. My swearing in was held on January 17, 2017, at the Whitaker Center in downtown Harrisburg. I took the stage with people I had met along the way, whose stories and struggles and hopes carried me to that moment. They were some of the people who shaped my campaign, my thinking, my goals. Their stories fueled my campaign and set the tenor for my term.

I wanted to have a mother whose daughter had been addicted to opioids up there with me, seniors who had been the victims of scams, families impacted by gun violence up with me because these were some of the most impactful stories I heard as I spent time in each city and town and county throughout the campaign. I carried their pain. I could never do their losses justice, but I did know just how impactful their willingness to be raw and honest had been for me as I formed my own agenda and priorities and opinions. On the day I knew I would have such a large audience as I laid out my vision for the Commonwealth, I wanted the attention to be on their words, so that folks in Pennsylvania would get the privilege of feeling with them, of praying for them, of coming together around them, and understanding the importance of the work we were about to do. Show up in a community that's forgotten, listen to the people who don't get an audience, and carry their emotional burden around with me and get shit done for them. Listen, feel, do.

Throughout that campaign, when I would visit other parts of the state and talk about combatting gun violence—especially in rural areas, where the realities of the issue aren't as present in their day-to-day lives—I would tell the stories of the moms and grandmas I'd heard from. I'd share their stories and their anguish and pain and fear and frustration with the system and desperation to change it so that no other mother will have to endure what they live with. We need to make sure their babies get home to them at night, I would tell them. We can do that in a way that doesn't interfere with your ability to hunt or protect yourself or to exercise your rights.

*   *   *

A day after I took my hand off the Bible in Harrisburg, Trump was sworn in in Washington. I never imagined the chaos that would come so immediately after Trump's inauguration. I didn't foresee having to sue the President of the United States, let alone sue him within days of him getting sworn in, let alone sue him more than two dozen times over the course of his first administration.

I was sworn in right around when Trump started talking about the so-called Muslim ban on foreign travel. In our office, we had discussed how we would handle the theoretical idea, but we figured that it was, at the very least, just bluster, and at most, something that his administration would work through some sort of process.

It was important to me in that first week to be present at home as much as I could. I wanted my kids to feel like I was still going to show up for them, too, even though I was now representing a bigger swath of folks in the Commonwealth. They'd gotten used to me being at home most nights as county commissioner, and, with the exception of the AG campaign, I'd gotten used to these rhythms and rituals, too. It was a constant balancing act. That week, it meant showing up for Shabbat, as I always did. By that Friday evening, as my family and I sat down for dinner, dozens of people had been held at airports across the country after Trump had issued an executive order to ban travel from seven Muslim-majority countries and halt refugees from entering the US. Political leaders from Pennsylvania ran to the airport in Philadelphia where a protest took shape. I monitored it all from home, observing Shabbat with the family. Protests erupted around the country through the weekend, and by Saturday, a federal judge in New York had issued a temporary stay on the order and ruled that all the people being held should be released. It was chaos.

I had been in the job for less than a week, and at home, I was trying to keep it as calm and steady as possible. I didn't want my kids to think that every week was going to be as insane as they did ultimately turn out to be. Honestly, maybe I was trying to convince myself of that, too. I was trying to keep our schedule as normal as possible, even as we held on to the weight of what was unfolding and went through the legal processes. By Sunday, that meant showing up as our boys' basketball coach in our local hoops league, as I did every week in the winter. I played in this league when I was a kid, and it was so special for me to now be able to coach my kids on the same court.

Here's the thing about my coaching: Without question or hesitation, I am a kind, gentle, supportive team leader to any kid I've ever coached. On the outside, I am encouraging. I hand out attaboys left and right. I'm cheering for their wins and assuaging their losses all the same—the makes and the misses. On the inside, I'm a freaking lunatic. Inwardly, I am boiling when the play breaks down, when they fail to set a proper pick or when they don't play aggressive defense or make the extra pass. I can't help my thoughts, but I do manage to control my actions. I would come home from the games mentally exhausted, and Lori would just laugh in my face when I would recount each play, each pass, each basket.

"They're seven-year-olds," she'd say.

She never understood how I could seemingly not be stressed from work but coaching a group of first- and second-graders could wind me up.

I was in the middle of all of this with these elementary school kids on the court and I could feel my iPhone buzzing nonstop. The ban was now real, and a group of fellow Democratic attorneys general from around the country had started talking about pushing back. Washington was the first state to sue the administration. I then organized a coalition of fifteen state attorneys general to file an amicus brief supporting the lawsuit.

Between calling the plays for the kids, I was texting with my fellow AGs. We didn't even have a team set up for this internally yet. None of us were fully prepared for this. It was extremely important for me that we follow the law, not the outrage cycle.

Don't get me wrong: there was so much to be outraged by. An overwhelming amount of real, and really damaging, horrific stuff was coming out of that administration in those first few days. And we were extremely fortunate that they were as sloppy as they were, because some of the procedural mistakes that they made in enacting the early executive orders bought us time.

After we won the first case, the administration came back with a revised mandate. I decided that I was not going to sue them again on this. The administration's revised mandate was more limited, and our lawyers felt we didn't have a strong case, so this was a legal decision, not a political one. And it made me one of the only Democratic AGs not to jump in to file a second suit right away.

I opposed the ban completely. I thought it was a horrible, offensive policy, for a whole host of reasons. But I also believed that it was technically legal. The President was within his legal right that second time. I was not going to oppose him just to oppose him. I wasn't going to sue him for the sake of it. My job isn't to sue the guy because I disagree with him or dislike him; I can and would only sue him if what he was doing was illegal.

And there was plenty of that to go around. My team and I sued him dozens of times over those four years, from the Muslim ban to access to birth control to environmental regulations. I felt good about those suits and the wins, but I got slammed at times from the resistance for not taking on every fight or joining every lawsuit.

I wasn't worried about what people on social media were going to say about me. My team and I focused on the law. I let that be my guide. You can't be your highest and best self if you are making decisions based on the boom-and-bust praise cycles of the internet. I needed to stay true to my guiding principles, not the whims of social media, if I wanted to get this right.

The only feedback that mattered to me was, first, the verdicts. If I was winning the suit I filed, I knew I was doing my job. And I was. And second, I was continuing to show up for the people I was representing—in areas that didn't vote for me and supported Trump just as much and as often as I did in areas that I knew were true blue. I showed up and treated everyone with respect. I told them how I was fighting for them. I listened to what they needed—whether that was to get money back from scammers or holding drug companies accountable for the fentanyl crisis or honoring any number of the commitments I had made to them. They knew that I was working for them, and that even though they supported Trump, they knew that I was being fair and judicious in the way I was handling my authority. I didn't hide the fact that I wasn't for the guy. I didn't hide the fact that I was a Democrat. But I tried not to take the bait. I had built up real relationships with people across the Commonwealth, because we listened to each other. I cared about them, and they knew that.

I was able to show them that I am going to show up. And I'm going to listen when I do. And, from there, I'm going to do something.

CHAPTER III

Your Word Against G-d's

"I'VE GOT TWO COOKIES AND cream, a mint chocolate chip, two cookie doughs, and chocolate," our server called out as she handed us the ice cream we waited a year for. I'd spent much of our twelve-and-a-half-hour ride packed into our minivan waiting to enjoy this. Every August, our extended family meets for this end-of-summer, pre-start-of-school trip in Hilton Head, South Carolina. It always includes a stop at the Salty Dog. It's an institution on the water with live music every night and bumper stickers that read, "If you ain't the lead dog, the scenery never changes." I like this phrase and place so much that I keep one of their stickers on a shelf in my office.

I didn't think I was going to make it down there that summer. It was August 2018. I was a year and a half into my term as Attorney General and at the fulcrum of the most consequential and emotionally grueling professional moment in my career.

The AG's office had been investigating the Catholic Church for sexual abuse and their cover-ups since before I was sworn in to the role in 2017, but the grand jury case had ballooned into a years-long monster of a case. It spanned six dioceses, which accounted for fifty-four of Pennsylvania's sixty-seven counties. The grand jury heard the testimony from dozens of witnesses concerning clergy sex abuse. It subpoenaed and reviewed half a million pages of internal diocesan documents, some of which were so gruesome and disturbing that I struggled to see the light as we uncovered what happened. There were credible allegations against more than three hundred priests. The grand jury found that there were more than a thousand children as victims, though they ultimately concluded that the real number was much higher, well into the many thousands.

The grand jury presented its findings and made its recommendations on the last day of April, some three months earlier. We'd been fighting since then to make sure that all 884 pages of their report would be made public. My team and I wanted the names of the individuals who perpetrated these crimes and those many who covered them up for decades to come to light. More than anything, we wanted the victims, many of whom I'd met at that point, who had held on to the weight of their trauma and bravely shared their harrowing stories, to know that it was not all for nothing, that we wouldn't be another of the many systems and institutions and people in power who would fail them and not bring them justice. They wanted the report out there. I wouldn't stop until it was.

By the end of the summer, I was on a razor's edge, waiting on the Pennsylvania Supreme Court to rule on when the report would be released and whether or not we would get to name the priests who abused these innocent children and the people who covered it all up—something that the Catholic Church and their lawyers were fighting tooth and nail.

I had told Lori that I didn't know if I would be able to go to Hilton Head, though I couldn't really explain why. Grand jury matters are, of course, secret. Nothing that is in front of that court can be taken outside. But keeping a tight hold held particular weight, in that office and in that moment. My predecessor in the role, Kathleen Kane, resigned after a special counsel concluded that secret grand jury information had been leaked to the *Philadelphia Daily News* by someone in her office. She was ultimately found guilty of seven misdemeanors and two felony counts of perjury in 2016 and served time in prison.

Needless to say, I was sensitive to my obligations. Even though working on this investigation tore at my insides and broke my heart every single day. It was load testing me—in humanity and decency, in institutions, and, honestly, in my faith.

*   *   *

I have confidence in my ability to understand very tough issues and to make the right call. There's a process to it. I obsessively read about whatever is in front of me. I surround myself with people who know their stuff. I ask an inordinate number of questions (just the way Carl Levin taught me). I assemble groups of internal and external experts on the subject matter at hand. I call on the handful of people who are my personal North Stars, Lori chief among them, along with a very small group of people whose judgment I trust and seek and who know how to guide me. I over-prepare on the facts, continually listen, call on the people who lead you to your center, and then execute. I practice that on a loop.

With the grand jury secrecy on this case, though, I was walled off from some of the most important people in positions of authority in my life when I needed their guidance most. I needed them more than I ever had, because of the agonizing details and degree of evil that was in every document and all the testimony, and the fact that these were innocent children, up against a powerful system that would spare no penny to absolve itself, even if it meant weaponizing G-d against them. I was keenly aware of just how rightly distrusting these victims were of people in positions of authority like me and governmental institutions like the one I represented, because nearly every single person in power until now had either not believed them, blamed them, or not brought them any justice. Many of the perpetrators were still out there, and as long as they were, as long as the cycle of abuse and cover-up remained secret and unchecked, there were more children who were potentially in harm's way.

This case was uphill from the start. The defense lawyers were ruthless. Many instances of the abuse took place years if not decades earlier, so evidence and statutes of limitations would make it extremely difficult not only to investigate but also to ultimately bring charges and justice. There were so many moments where we questioned if the avenue we were taking was the best to get the truth out and hold people accountable, or, if we were stuck at a particular impasse, how we could break through.

The saving grace for me was that I had an incredible staff around me, not only because they were such hyper-skilled, hardworking lawyers and investigators, but also because we were all in the foxhole together. This team was the core of everything for me, particularly Michelle Henry, my first deputy, Jen Selber, my executive deputy, and Dan Dye, the lead prosecutor on the investigation. They are among the most talented, caring, and capable people I've ever had the privilege to work with. We spent more and more time in the office together, because the case was so onerous, and keeping it confidential felt almost like living a double life. Holding all of the pressure and darkness to ourselves was getting more difficult to do. Every day, I was pushing my team harder and harder to get at the truth. To be clear, they didn't need any extra motivation—they were working seemingly 24/7 to uncover the truth. As decision points came closer, as the opposition around us got stronger, I tried to shoulder the burden of risk from my staff so they were unshackled and able to pursue justice without limitation.

I prayed for clarity constantly. I prayed and I prayed and I prayed. I tried to leave it at the office. It's a practice I have become quite good at, this kind of compartmentalization. You kind of need to compartmentalize in order to do this kind of work and also be able to show up at home. What I have learned is that I have to prioritize work that needs to be done and tune out the rest, and then leave the difficulties of the day behind by the time I head home to be present with my kids. This has gotten harder, to be sure, as my responsibilities have grown. I've made about a million LEGO cities and sat in gyms and on sidelines for games, and in seats for the school plays (that I never saw Sophia in because she was the stage manager) in the midst of these particularly trying periods at work. I still show up for my kids and I'm home every Friday for Shabbat no matter what I've got going on at the office and what is demanding my attention or time. My kids didn't ask for any of this. They're the priority for me, and knowing that they know they're the most important thing to me is the whole game as a parent. But it's gotten more challenging to lock in on them as the amount of external pressure has ramped up.

During that clergy abuse investigation, my role called for me to become subsumed by the case, in secret. I would be lying if I said I wasn't periodically consumed by it. There were days where I was all in with my kids, and then there were other days where I was completely withdrawn. I would be present, but I couldn't shake the darkness and the details I was steeped in from the investigation. There were a few times that I lunged across the room to grab my iPhone from Lori or the kids looking for an innocuous photo or trying to put on music, in fear that they might see something that would draw them into that awful darkness.

So by the end of the summer, as the annual Hilton Head trip neared, I was looking forward to a break from it all and some quality time with my family. I also didn't want Lori to make that long drive by herself. By the end of July, the Supreme Court ruled that the interim report and various responses would have to be released by August 8. If there were challenges, they would have to be dealt with so the report would come out by no later than 2 p.m. on August 14. So we knew that was the last possible second that the report would come out. And my family was leaving for Hilton Head on the eleventh. For weeks I'd been pushing off giving Lori an answer about my plans and my timing. By the time we sat down for Shabbat dinner on the tenth without any more clarity, I decided that I'd drive down with them the following morning and I'd head back for the deadline on the fourteenth.

When we got our ice cream at the Salty Dog, everything to everyone else was as it always was. We'd play the same beach games, bunk in the same house, eat too much of the same ice cream, and body surf for hours in the waves, hoping to miss the jellyfish stings that seemed to come in those late August warm Carolina waters. We would ride bikes in the morning, the kids in charge of where we would end up. Our skin would be sticky with salt and sand and sunscreen. It would be our timeworn, happy mess. No one else was carrying the weight of my other reality, the one waiting for me as I checked my phone about a hundred times a day, desperate to find out if the report would all come to light.

The next day, I had to head back to Harrisburg so that I could be there if and when it was released. I still wasn't sure whether it would be hours or days, but I knew that soon, Lori would be able to read the report in full, to get why I was so rattled and not myself, so withdrawn, so gutted to my core.

"I'm sorry," I told Lori and the kids as I got into the car for the airport. They barely looked up from their fun as I drove away. Damn, I thought as I watched them laughing as they raced down to the water. I was torn up inside on every level—as a dad, as the Attorney General. While it hurt to leave at that moment, I witnessed my kids so happy, so together. I felt so blessed to be their dad, so fortunate to be Mr. Lori.

*   *   *

When you first take over as Attorney General, there are a number of investigations already in progress. Some of them are from your predecessor. Some from your predecessor's predecessor. There was so much to get up to speed on, so many cases in various forms of progress.

I wanted to know everything. For each separate investigation, we would try to devour as much as we could on the case, and then determine whether we wanted to continue to pursue it and put our resources and time toward prosecuting it. In those early weeks, we dug into the evidence and case files from morning until very late at night. We worked constantly, which made it easy and quick to build a real trust and affection for the team around me. They all had different expertise and came from all sorts of backgrounds, but I was surrounded and supported by a group that knew how to handle this, in a way that I hadn't quite experienced. They had the abilities and the track records that I didn't. They filled my gaps, and I filled some of theirs. Their knowledge and abilities gave me the confidence that when they'd brief me or explain things to me or take on areas of cases, I would have all of the information and ability to make the right judgment call based on everything they showed me. We worked nonstop. We took it really seriously. We understood the weight of our work. We were committed. We needed to get these things right.

The role as prosecutor was all new to me. Most attorneys general spend years arguing cases in courtrooms before they get here. I was learning the ropes and getting up to speed on these investigations, and the only way I knew how was by overpreparing, for every meeting, for every phone call, even if they were just with my team. I immersed myself in every case. I studied them. I hired people smarter than me who had more experience than I did, and I learned from them. I didn't just want to sign off on a wiretap—which was something I had never done before. I wanted to get super granular on the process, to understand every detail of how it worked, to be walked through each step, so I would come to my own conclusions confidently. I wanted to lead by listening, by doing, by putting in the work.

Not all of it was unfamiliar. A number of the investigations we inherited involved trauma and abuse to children, and I was drawn to leaning in on these cases. I am certain it has to do with the house in which I grew up and what I learned from my parents. I was more sensitive, more inclined to find the bad actors and hold them accountable, to seek justice for all those who suffered, to take the broken pieces and people and do my part to make them whole.

I thought about my dad a lot, who, as a pediatrician, often served as an expert witness on behalf of the Commonwealth in child sex abuse cases, examining victims and lending his knowledge to prosecutors as they went after child predators.

When I was serving as state representative, two of the prosecutors who often called on my dad as a witness opened Pennsylvania's first child advocacy center, Mission Kids. Typically, when an incident is reported, a child has to go to a police station to detail their allegations to a police officer, then to be examined by a doctor, where they had to recount the story again and oftentimes to another office to visit with a therapist. That tough process can often feel like part of the abuse itself. Bright and cheerful-looking, Mission Kids, on the other hand, is a softer place to land. Children are interviewed by someone trained to talk to kids. Law enforcement, prosecutors, social workers, and other professionals watch the interview on a closed circuit, so they have everything they need to aid in prosecution, without putting undo stress on these victims. They're then connected with trusted mental health professionals and doctors to guide them toward their healing. It all happens under one caring roof for these children. I was able to help Mission Kids get a grant in order to build a new facility. Since they opened their doors, they have conducted more than sixty-five hundred forensic interviews and made sixteen hundred mental health referrals.

I took this focus to the county commissioner's office once I learned how inefficient our office of children and youth was functioning. When I took office, the way it would work was that every day, those employees would drive to the office in Norristown, receive a paper packet of which houses they were to visit that day, drive all over the county in order to conduct their assessments and visits, and then drive back to the office to write a report. These child welfare workers were not only burning hours on each side of their day driving to and from the office, but then they would spend a couple of hours on top of that doing data entry. And by the time they were doing that data entry, they were hours out from their initial interviews. They couldn't possibly have the information as fresh in their minds.

I asked our IT folks why they couldn't just log on to tablets from home in the morning, get their list of houses to go to for the day, drive directly there, and then immediately input their notes. They could, they answered. As soon as we implemented it, we increased effectiveness. The number of houses they were able to visit skyrocketed. The information was more accurate because it was recorded in real time. Kids were better looked after. The switch was simple and obvious, but no one had taken the time to look at the problem, to think of how to better serve these people, to execute a common-sense solution.

So while the courtroom terrain was unfamiliar to me, I'd long been primed to look out for kids in traumatic moments and challenging situations. During the clergy abuse investigation, we had started investigating Dr. Johnnie Barto, a near-seventy-year-old pediatrician with offices in Cambria and Somerset counties, for indecent assault, corruption of minors, and endangering the welfare of children. The case came to our office in 2017, after Barto excused a mother from the exam room in order to examine her twelve-year-old son's genitals. She had brought him in to see Dr. Barto, the trusted pediatrician in this rural community, because he was suffering from the flu. The mother, obviously bewildered and uncomfortable with the visit, opened the door to see the doctor fondling her son. She immediately confronted him, but he walked away and offered no explanation. She reported the incident to local police, and the case came to my desk.

We announced charges in early 2018, and I held a press conference saying that we believed there might be other victims, and that we wanted them to know we will listen to them, believe them, and prosecute any offender to the fullest extent of the law, no matter who they are or how powerful they may seem. I made a point to do this, because, in a case like this, there are often many more victims living in the shadows and afraid to come forth. I want them to know they will be heard, believed, and backed.

This was no exception. It was a domino effect. By March, we announced additional charges against Dr. Barto for assaulting a fourteen-year-old family relative and repeatedly abusing another family relative, a seven-year-old girl. The assaults, which began when the victim was three years old, took place over the course of years.

Despite the multiple sets of charges and our belief that the abuse was even more widespread, some in the community came after me. Dr. Barto had been a pediatrician for decades in the town. He was on the school board. Some in the community thought my office was making this up. That the guy they knew couldn't possibly have done anything like this. One afternoon, in a local Panera where I was grabbing a quick bite to eat before we announced a new round of charges, a neighborhood guy recognized me and approached me, shaking his head. "You're all wrong about this guy," he said. "You're going to regret this."

By the summer, more than twenty-five victims with credible accounts of assault had come forward, spanning several decades. In some instances, unaware parents were in the same room where the abuse took place. I met with several of the victims privately. I couldn't shake their despair, maybe because my dad was a trusted community pediatrician, or that I had four young kids of my own. I was crushed by the ways in which they'd pushed down their abuse and carried the burden of their secret. That the shameful actions of a predator became their shame; that a person they'd trusted to ease their pain caused irrevocable harm. In 2019, Dr. Barto was convicted and sentenced to up to 158 years in prison for what he did. I sat in the front row of the courtroom to witness his sentencing. In six years as Attorney General, that was the only sentencing I ever made a point to attend in person.

*   *   *

Until I became AG, much of my work had existed on a continuum of listen, feel, do. I spent a tremendous amount of time with constituents listening to stories about their pain points. Sometimes that had to do with the cost of health care or access to good doctors. Schools without enough funding. Nursing homes without proper staffing. Parents of children with special needs not getting the support the government owed them. Public dollars not being used in the right places. When I was running for state representative, I knocked on all of those doors to hear about those issues from the people I wanted to serve. When I was in office there, I did those town halls—about fifteen a year—to keep that connection, so I'd know what needs had to be met.

Even now, I'll have someone come up to me when I'm in a sporting goods store with one of my kids, or they'll approach Lori in the grocery store to tell us that they're having an issue applying for a permit or getting reimbursed from an insurer for their husband's care. I make sure that my team looks into the problem, and then report back to me as soon as it's handled.

That's the whole reason to be in this kind of job. It's why I want to serve, why I felt called to it all those years ago, and why I keep going. It feeds me to do all of these constituent services and to make this world and people's lives a little better. In that, I find the light.

I was having a really hard time finding it, though, in those early months cranking through these child abuse cases as AG. When we first dug into the Catholic Church investigation that began under the prior Attorney General, we could tell right away that it was the tip of the iceberg, with an ever-growing number of victims. There was no indication of the scale and breadth that this would expand into. Our minds didn't have the capacity to imagine the degree of evil.

It took about six or seven months to begin to see the magnitude of the case. Victim after victim would come in and share their story. To hear these individuals, who'd held on to their trauma, who'd have it seep into every crevice in their lives, cracked my team open. These families had been ripped apart, their innocence shattered. Many of them struggled to have normal relationships, to show any kind of affection or belief in G-d. Some of them had turned to drugs as a means to cope. Many victims didn't survive, taking their own lives as their despair proved too grave.

With every bit of testimony, of digging, the case snowballed. From the testimony, we determined that when these incidents were reported to various dioceses, they would make notes and document them. The details would be memorialized in memos. The dioceses wrote it all down. And then they'd just file it away in what they called "secret archives." In some diocesan offices, the archives existed in regular old filing cabinets. The church's Code of Canon Law specifically requires each diocese to maintain such an archive. Typically, the bishop has the key. As soon as we learned this, I authorized search warrants to get as many documents from these secret archives as we possibly could.

What resulted was half a million documents. We reviewed them all, as did the grand jury. All of this was shocking, having nothing to do with what we found, because it is almost too evil to believe that not only did they get reports of these many thousands of abuse cases, but they recorded them, and kept them, for decades on end. And they did nothing about them. They made a point not to share their secret files with law enforcement.

You have to believe that you are above the law in order to purposely keep evidence of crimes and their cover-ups. You have to feel there's no way you will get caught or face any kind of punishment. And, frankly, until that point, why would they believe otherwise? The system had worked for these bad actors to continue their bad acting without the threat of consequences. The Catholic Church has more money than perhaps any other entity in the world. Some would argue it has more power too. In their view, the Church didn't have to respond to local law enforcement because they answered to G-d. Their policies from the Vatican expressly directed them to ignore law enforcement and handle matters internally. In their way of thinking about this, if a parent or a victim comes forward with an allegation, and they respond by shifting blame, shaming the victim, deflecting the parents' rage and concern, then writing it down and filing it away into the archive, that means they've dealt with it.

We went through, allegation by allegation, document by document. The stories were harrowing. As a warning to readers, this part is as graphic as it is grueling. If you aren't ready to read these details, I get it. Skip ahead. But it's as important for me to retell these victims' truth today as it was when I was prosecuting the case, so that the scope and depths of these crimes and the pain they caused can be truly understood.

In the Grand Jury Report, there were the allegations against Monsignor Thomas J. Benestad of the Diocese of Allentown. A victim reported that he had been sexually abused from 1981 through 1993, starting when he was nine years old. Correspondence showed that the diocese reported the allegation to the Northampton County District Attorney's Office, which conducted an investigation and found the victim's allegations to be credible. In a statement to the Northampton County detectives, the victim said that his first memory of abuse happened while he attended CCD class at St. Bernard's, where Benestad was assigned. The victim was taken out of class by a nun and brought to Benestad in his office because he had worn shorts to CCD, which was against the rules. Benestad told him that his attire was sinful, and instructed him to get on his knees and start praying. That's when Benestad unzipped his pants and told the victim to perform oral sex on him. The nine-year-old did as he was told. Benestad also performed oral sex on the victim. The victim recalled that after the abuse, Benestad would bring out a clear bottle of holy water and squirt it into the victim's mouth to purify him. The district attorney's office found the applicable statute of limitations had expired and no charges were brought against Benestad, and even though additional complaints had been made against him, the diocese elected to rely on Benestad's denial of all allegations. Rather than remove Benestad from their ministry, they granted him retirement in Boca Raton, where he assisted with a local parish.

We uncovered a ring of priests in the Diocese of Pittsburgh who shared information about victims among themselves. One victim, "George," testified in front of the grand jury that he had grown up and loved the church, as he attended Catholic school for twelve years and served as an altar boy on the city's South Side. One priest, George Zirwas, befriended him, taught him how to drive, and took him away on vacations. He began introducing him to his "friends," fellow priests who brought him to their rectory and ordered him to stand on a bed. They drew an analogy to the image of Christ on the cross and told "George" to remove his shirt. After that, the abuse began, and the priests gave him a big gold cross to wear around his neck. According to corroborating evidence found within diocesan records, these crosses, which were given to other victims as well, were designations that these children had been abused already—a badge of sorts to alert other predatory priests that these children had been subject to sexual abuse and were prime targets for more victimization.

In another instance in the Grand Jury Report, a kind, warm family embraced their new priest, Father Augustine Giella, when he moved to the St. John the Evangelist Church in Enhaut in 1983. Almost as immediately, he began abusing five of the family's eight daughters, and later, other relatives in the family. The sisters testified before the grand jury detailing the abuse, which included collecting samples of the sisters' urine, pubic hair, and menstrual blood with a device he applied to the toilet. Some of the samples he collected he would ingest.

All of this could have been stopped much earlier, had the Diocese of Harrisburg acted in 1987 on a complaint made to a teacher at their school, which made its way up the diocesan chain, the evidence showed. No action was taken until one twelve-year-old victim found nude photos of herself in Giella's residence. The family then went to the police, who executed search warrants. In his home, they found a young girl's panties, plastic containers containing pubic hairs identified by initials, twelve vials of urine, used feminine sanitary products, and photographs of girls in sexually explicit positions. Giella was arrested in August 1992, and admitted his actions to the police. He died awaiting trial.

Before their testimony, the sisters could barely share the details of their own abuse with each other, because they were terrified of what they would learn. The youngest sister, the one who finally reported Giella's criminal conduct, had a panic attack while in the grand jury suite. "I believe in G-d," she said. "But I don't go to church. My son is the only reason I'm alive. Thank G-d I had him, because if I didn't have him, I probably would have killed myself a long time ago." In speaking with her and my special agent involved in the case, she expressed her overwhelming fear that nothing had been done in the months since she'd testified before the grand jury. She was concerned that the grand jury had been stopped, that I had abandoned my fight for her and for the other victims—perhaps because the church had silenced them, or we didn't believe them. That the truth would never be made public, she feared.

I understood why she felt that. If you were a victim and you courageously came to testify in front of the grand jury, you did so on your own, without any knowledge of anyone else testifying. You didn't know how you fit into the larger case or even if there was a wider aperture to the abuse. We knew that there were so many others coming forward. We were aware of just how hard we were pushing, how many documents we'd subpoenaed, how many interviews we were compiling. But because of the secrecy rules, the victims knew little more about the investigation beyond their trauma. And because we were going so aggressively, compiling so much evidence, and conducting so much testimony in the grand jury room, months could go by after their testimony and there would be no outward signs of progress, even though in reality we were chipping away at this gigantic iceberg of a case.

These are folks who had been let down by their priests, their families, their police, their G-d. Why wouldn't they believe that they were now being let down by their Attorney General? They'd call our lead investigator and ask if we'd been corrupted by the church. You told us that if we shared our truth, we could trust you, they'd tell us. We did, and nothing happened, the same way nothing has ever happened.

That crushed me. The reality couldn't have been further from that.

For a year and a half, we had been absorbing their pain and working nonstop. Michelle, Jen, Dan and the whole team were all in to uncover the truth and hold people accountable. We were going to court arguing in front of these judges trying to make sure the truth would come out and these victims would be heard. Even still, and as much as we were pushing forward, we were being thwarted by the opposition.

I struggled to find that common ground with the lawyers who lined up on the other side to represent the church in order to stop the truth from coming out. I am good about keeping my personal emotions in check at work. Not personalizing the fights. But I am the first to admit that their lack of integrity got under my skin. Maybe that's a polite way of saying I got angry. Really, really angry.

The grand jury finalized its report at the end of April, but the church was battling to keep it from public view. Here's how that report began:

"We, the members of the Grand Jury, need you to hear this. We know some of you have heard some of it before. There have been other reports about sex abuse within the Catholic Church. But never on this scale. For many of us, those earlier stories happened someplace else, someplace away. Now we know the truth: it happened everywhere . . . We are not satisfied by the few charges we can bring, which represent only a tiny percentage of all the child abusers we saw. We are sick over all the crimes that will go unpunished and uncompensated. This report is our only recourse."

The fact that I didn't have the typical prosecutorial experience as Attorney General meant that I approached cases from a different vantage point. The exceptional prosecutors around me tended to be a little more small "c" conservative, more constrained. I was, as my staff will attest, aggressive and willing to push and not conform to the way it has always been done.

My main concern was signaling to the victims that we were moving. Until now, they had no way of knowing that the investigation had even continued, let alone that there was a finalized report.

We were able to arrest one priest at the beginning of May for whom the statute of limitations on the abuse had not run out.

This at least meant that the press could report that the investigation had continued and some progress was being made. But I wanted to go further.

I remembered reviewing the testimony of Erie Bishop Lawrence Persico in front of the grand jury. He had taken over for one of the worst bishops in this cover-up, and I just had a feeling that he wanted to be on the right side of this.

I told my staff that I wanted to meet him, one on one. If I could get him to say that he supported releasing the report publicly, not only would it create a fissure among the bishops and put pressure on them to do right, but it would also let the victims know that a report existed and we were mounting a case to have it released.

My team informed me that I was totally nuts. He'd never go for it. He had lawyers. He had already testified. We had never met before. Why would he ever agree to sit down with me to talk about something he obviously wanted to stay away from?

I knew he would have to have counsel present. That was fine by me. I pushed and I pushed. By mid-May, he agreed. He asked when we could schedule it and where. "How about right now?" I said. I flew to Erie with Dan Dye, my very able lead prosecutor. I didn't even want to waste time in a car. We met in a room at the small Erie airport.

"I know we are in the middle of this," I said. "But there is a broader, deeper moment for us here. Both of our faiths teach us to care for children, those less fortunate, those who are more vulnerable. This is a chance for you to live that out." It didn't take much beyond that for him to agree, though he expressed concerns about how he would catch grief from his fellow bishops. Before we went our separate ways, I couldn't resist. "How do these guys do this?" I asked. "They abuse these kids or they cover the abuse up, and then they go on to preach about helping kids on Sundays."

"We compartmentalize," he said. "Priests are very good at that."

Persico released a statement following our meeting saying that we had met to discuss the grand jury's report, and that he had informed me that he would "forgo any legal challenges to the grand jury process and its work."

"I realize that the Grand Jury Report will contain information that will be difficult for all of us to hear, but in order for us to focus on the future, we have to have a solid knowledge of the past," he said.

*   *   *

"What's this about a grand jury report?" Lori asked me the following morning, as the statements made their way into the news. It was really the first time that I could mention the case at all to her, which felt like somewhat of a relief.

"You have no idea," I said. She didn't. She couldn't.

With it out there now that there was in fact a report, I told my team that I wanted to invite the victims to my office. I knew we couldn't say anything about the contents of the report until the court approved its release, but I wanted them to meet each other and get a chance to talk to us, to see that we were working and that we gave a damn.

Again, they told me that I was pushing too hard. That I was limited in what I would be able to say. That they might not even want to meet with me, because they were so upset by the lack of public progress and because they didn't trust that anyone in power would actually do something for them. I just kept saying that if they could read between the lines and walk away feeling a little less pain, with a little more patience and faith that something could come from this, then we would keep fighting in court to get this report released without the pressure of victims thinking we shelved their truths.

So we invited about two dozen of the victims to my office. We arranged a whole bunch of chairs around my conference table to form a circle and all squeezed in together. I am sure these folks came into this day not knowing what exactly to expect, though

I'm sure no one held particularly high hopes. More of the same was likely the best they anticipated.

Several of the victims had never met each other before. They came from all different parts of the state, all different parishes and churches. Some of them were young and some of them were in their eighties. Some had voted for me; some had not, which they weren't shy about sharing with me.

That's just fine, I said. I am here working for you, no matter what. All of them had been burdened by the secrets they'd kept. I wanted to make those loads lighter.

We sat around that table for hours that day. It was, without question, the most impactful and emotional meeting I've ever been part of in my entire time in public service.

Many of the victims shared their stories. Several didn't. Each one was a gut punch, even though I had read their testimonies from the grand jury room. The parents of a young boy who had been raped so aggressively that his back broke. The pain was so unmanageable that he got hooked on OxyContin and ultimately died of a heroin overdose. One woman told us that while she was being raped as a preteen, the priest would tell her she didn't matter, that G-d said she didn't matter.

To see their faces and look them in the eye as they recounted these absolute horrors was beyond the words I can put on this page. And to see how their faith had been so weaponized in order to continue the abuse—to mark a victim with a gold cross so they could be a target for other predators; to wash a child's mouth out with holy water after you assaulted him; to tell a young girl that G-d said he could abuse her because she wasn't special—these are not stories you could brush aside and keep believing in the system. Or keep believing, period.

They questioned me about whether we would release the report and what was in it. They asked what we were doing, if we had abandoned them, if the Pope had gotten to us and convinced us not to move forward. All I could tell them was that we heard them, we cared deeply, and that we were working harder than they knew. At the end of the day, I told them that I hoped they would be able to see just how hard we all worked to make sure their truth would be shared.

I walked out of that meeting with a renewed fire burning within me. This report was going to get out there. My team and I wouldn't stop until it did.

*   *   *

"You should just get in touch with the Pope," Lori told me that summer, still not knowing its contents but knowing how important it was to me to do right by the victims.

Our work to release the report pushed forward during the summer of 2018, mostly in confidential ways, but there was another leak in the press about the continued opposition by the church to keep the report from ever seeing the light of day.

Sure! Just like that! I'll ring him up on his little papal hotline— 1–800-VATICAN—and tell him he should just release the report! I can't believe I hadn't thought of that!

She's crazier than I am, I thought.

"Don't you remember that you met him a few years ago? He might remember that."

I was pretty sure our meeting in 2015 wouldn't exactly ring any bells for him. Pope Francis had come to Saint Charles Borromeo Seminary in Montgomery County, where he was staying during the World Meeting of Families in Philadelphia. I was county commissioner at the time, and in all my time in public service, I had learned some valuable lessons, among them that you should just kind of hang around like you belong. I also wanted to soak in the magnitude of the moment, just being near the Pope felt like a once-in-a-lifetime experience that I would hold on to. I knew I was going to have the honor of meeting and greeting him and welcoming him officially to Montgomery County. I was placed at the base of the steps for when he emerged from his tiny Fiat Popemobile. But once the thirty-second greet was over, my job was kind of complete. He walked up the steps and into the seminary. I knew this was an historic moment, so I stayed put and I followed the Pope. Inside, he spoke quietly to a small group assembled in the lobby. I watched from about fifteen feet away. I'd rarely thought about it since. Now, Lori had remembered that this Pope had spoken about the victims of abuse in the way that had broken with the past. Maybe he would be open to this, too.

"That's not how this works," I said. We cleaned up dinner, did the normal ritual of putting the house back together after a day of kids tearing it up and then got into bed.

Only I couldn't sleep. I was overtired, and this was a particularly trying period. I was still walled off from Lori, even though she knew bits and pieces from what was out there. I was traveling across the state to sit down with more victims to offer my support and hear from them. I had their stories and all that they carried constantly playing on a loop. I had just recently visited the home of an eighty-three-year-old veteran, Bob Corby, who was abused in the late 1940s by his priest, and had been so scarred that he asked me to move to another seat in his cramped living room because he didn't feel comfortable sharing the couch with an adult male. He explained how hard it was to show affection to his wife, or hug his children, or see male doctors or psychologists. I had to do right by him.

At the same time, our court battles intensified. The church's counsel had been arguing that releasing the report would violate the priests' constitutional reputational protections. We had argued that we would allow anyone named in the report unlimited and unedited space to respond to the allegations right in the report. We were awaiting a decision from Pennsylvania's Supreme Court.

That long, fitful night, I couldn't stop thinking about Lori's suggestion. Somehow, from the recesses of my mind, it came to me that the group Pope Francis had met with when I followed him into the seminary was a group of abuse survivors and their loved ones. I literally had not thought about our meeting once throughout this entire investigation. Now, I couldn't let it go.

So I got out of bed and onto my computer and started googling. I found a handful of sites that keep logs and minutes of every visit the Pope makes and every speech he gives. I unearthed a transcript of the remarks he gave that day at the seminary, when I hung around in the hall after shaking his hand that day in Montgomery County about three years earlier.

The remarks began: "I am deeply pained by the stories, the sufferings and the pain of minors who were sexually abused by priests," he said. "I continue to be ashamed that persons charged with the tender care of those little ones abused them and caused them grave harm. I deeply regret this. G-d weeps. The crimes and sins of sexual abuse of minors may no longer be kept secret; I commit myself to ensuring that the church makes every effort to protect minors and I promise that those responsible will be held to account."

I felt like I was dreaming. What were the odds? That I had been there the day the Pope had openly expressed the exact support for ending the exact secrecy I was fighting the church tooth and nail over? And that Lori somehow had gotten the madcap idea to tell me to write to him?

I guess I had no choice but to listen now.

*   *   *

As insane as it sounds, I sat down and wrote a letter to Pope Francis. I wrote of the coincidence. I told him that I had been moved by his words and his pledge to follow the path of truth wherever it may lead.

"Sadly," I wrote, "some of the clergy leading the church in Pennsylvania have failed to heed your words."

I wrote that our office had found widespread sexual abuse of children and a systemic cover-up by leaders of the church, and that I wanted to release the findings, but that petitioners implicated by the report were trying to stop me and stand in the way of truth in an effort to silence victims.

"Please call on them to 'follow the path of truth' you laid out and permit the healing process to begin," I wrote.

The trouble was, I didn't exactly know how to get this to the Pope, per se. This wasn't something I had done before. Was this something anyone had seriously done before? My team tested our luck by reaching out to the office of Callista Gingrich, who at the time was serving as the US ambassador to the Vatican, who told us they could get the letter to his staff. After a few days, we released the letter publicly, too. We knew that it would mount some pressure on the church and further signal to victims that we were trying to make good on our promise. It wasn't lost on me that this could light a fire under the Pennsylvania Supreme Court, too. It also ran the risk of pissing everyone off just as easily. But I knew that the more this was churning out there, the more difficult it would be for the Supreme Court not to let the public see the report.

It is unclear to this day if the Pope ever read my letter. But a few weeks after I sent it, I got a call from a childhood friend of his from Argentina, who was now a professor at St. Joseph's University, just outside of Philadelphia. He told me that my letter had been received.

*   *   *

With all of this building, it was getting to the point where I had to definitively say whether or not I could make it to our annual family time in Hilton Head. I'd been in this darkness, waiting for the final determination about when this report would be made public and how much would be redacted. Every day felt like a year. I still couldn't talk about the substance of the report with Lori. I needed to snap myself out of it and spend as much time as I could with the kids as the deadline that the court had set approached. So, for a day, I went.

That weekend, we officially got the order that the final version of the report could be released. It was up to us when and how.

I don't know that I have ever felt such relief. For the victims, foremost. This was their reckoning. That was the whole reason we started and continued and closed. Selfishly, I was desperate to talk to Lori about it. I had a year's worth of anguish that I needed to share. I hated holding these secrets. I wanted my way back to her light and partnership. I called her almost im-mediately after the court gave us the green light. Like, within seconds. The words flew out of my mouth. "Hey," I said. "So you're about to learn the difficult details why I've been acting like a maniac for the last year and a half and it's all going to be made public now."

I told her some of what was in there as I prepared to address the victims and the media.

I knew I was going to get attacked, and I understood why. Here I was, Attorney General, naming names and taking on powerful people within the very powerful Catholic Church. The reality is that Catholicism is a beautiful religion. And I am able to separate that beauty and the family that goes to church on Sunday and their relationship with their Catholic G-d from the organization behind the church, which we found to be corrupt. That organization was weaponizing that beautiful faith that is important to so many people. What these corrupt priests and bishops did was a slap in the face to the faithful. It was the very worst thing that you could do, to take something as sacred as that and pervert it.

After Lori and I hung up, I gathered myself and joined a group of victims we had invited to a press conference on the day we released the report. This was their day, their moment. Many of them had kept in touch after our meeting earlier that summer. My team and I were so moved by their accounts, by their words, by seeing the hurt of these events on their faces, that we knew that's how the news had to be delivered. We didn't want to sugarcoat a single word. We wanted to use the actual language of what happened. It had to be said out loud, to the public, in specifics, in their voices.

In fact, in the days leading up to the report's release, we were preparing for what we hoped would be an eventual public accounting. We wrote remarks that couldn't convey even a fraction of what we knew happened and the emotional weight of it all. As we described story after story and one horrific event after another, Michelle, my first deputy, turned to me and said, "I think the grand jury's words and the facts of these cases speak for themselves. I don't think we need to add any flair here, and I don't think we need to add any adjectives." Just the facts. Those were more than enough. So, working with Joe Grace, my communications director at the time, we scrubbed nearly every adjective from the remarks. There was no place or need for rhetoric. It was just the truth. And the truth should carry that day.

We wanted the victims to have that moment for their stories to be told. For accountability to finally come.

Their bravery was on full display as they sat with me on the stage as I outlined the horrors of what took place in Pennsylvania.

After the press conference wrapped, my team and I met up at a local hotel with the group of survivors who made the trip to the Capitol. I wanted to tell them that their bravery made this possible. That I understood why they'd lost faith in everything.

I had lost faith in so much, too. It's hard for me to say if this is exactly why it happened, but it was around this time that I found myself spending less and less time in a synagogue to observe my faith. To be clear, nothing bad had happened at my temple, or any other synagogue I've ever stepped foot in, to my knowledge. At the same time, I felt I needed a much closer relationship with my faith. It was a push and pull—of me needing my faith to lean on in order to get me through the most challenging period, and me questioning how G-d could let this happen to these innocent children.

I wanted the victims to know that I worked hard for them so they could live out the rest of their years knowing that the truth was finally shared, that sometimes institutions could be forces for good.

For my team, that's the reason we do these jobs in the first place. You return to the people, allow them to be your core. It's why we've continued to stay in touch with each other for all these years. A number of the victims get together to celebrate birthdays and milestones throughout the year, and I am lucky that they sometimes FaceTime me in so that I can join in with them. I make sure I call them on August 14 to check in.

One of the victims who had been abused as a young child and never had kids of his own as a result, recalled how the abuse "destroyed" him, that it was a "lifelong issue," and that working to bring justice to light in this case was "one of the proudest things I've ever done in my life."

One of the sisters who had been abused starting when she met the priest at nineteen months old, when she was still in diapers, said that with the truth out there, it would be refreshing not to have to pretend like she was someone else all the time.

"It's very lonely. Especially when it's your word against G-d's."

*   *   *

I took the first flight out to Hilton Head the morning after the report's release. I needed to hug my family. Truthfully, I couldn't wait.

"Daddy!" They ran up to me, collapsing their sandy little bodies into my arms. I was home, no longer alone.

Lori and I took a long walk on the beach once the kids were settled back in. I could feel my heart rate finally coming back down. And I told her about the victims and their unbelievable courage, the amazing team I felt privileged to work this case with. I said that this was likely the end of the road for me politically given how I anticipated this would land in the large Catholic community in Pennsylvania.

162 WHERE WE KEEP THE LIGHT

I really did believe this. I'd made my peace with being a one-term Attorney General, if it meant that I could put my head on the pillow at night knowing I did my job and made good for these victims.

"I think you are totally wrong," Lori said. "I really don't think you're losing anyone, least of all Catholics, because of this." I should have known at that moment what always bears out. That my wife knew better.

There is a certain peace to going down a road you know is right. You feel the conviction of it. You know the purpose. But while the path may be right, the outcome isn't certain. And if you're the one leading people down this harder, uncharted path, where the end point is unknown, there's a whole added layer of pressure and uncertainty. You are teetering on a high wire of risk, between reward and failure, darkness and light. You've got no one you can really talk to about it, because no one has been there before. You feel isolated, but not enough that you alone would bear the brunt of a defeat if it didn't pay off.

Thank G-d that for me that loneliness was not lasting. The risk paid off. The light, found.

*   *   *

When we lived in Washington and I was working on the Hill, we lived up by the National Cathedral, in Northwest DC. We would drive down Massachusetts Avenue, past all of the embassies and where the Vice President lives, onto Rock Creek Parkway. That was our route. Every day we'd ride past the Apostolic Nunciature of the Holy See (basically the embassy for the Vatican) on the route, and we would see a guy on the corner holding up different signs that had to do with pedophilia and the Catholic church.

Rain, snow, heat, hail—he was there. It was a fixture of our daily life that we'd note, though we never interacted with him.

When we left DC in 2003, we never saw him again. I don't think he ever came up between Lori and me again, either. But in the days following the release of the report, Lori called me at work.

"Remember that guy with the signs outside of the Vatican Embassy in DC?" she said. It was fifteen years earlier. We'd not talked about him since. And I had literally just been thinking about him and his signs. Of course what this guy was writing and protesting and trying to put out there had been true. Everyone just drove right by him, every day, for years—including me. No one seemingly did anything. He was begging people to listen, literally carrying the weight of the truth in his hands. But he had the conviction to try to get the message out and to find justice for the victims.

I knew that I had to reach him, to tell him that my team had done that. The trouble was, how on Earth was I going to find this guy? I knew nothing about him. I didn't live in DC. I had no idea if he was still out there every day. I obviously didn't know his name or his story or where he lived or worked.

So I googled him. I just typed in: "guy who stands out on Mass Ave. protesting Catholic Church." Straightaway, a story in the *Washingtonian* popped up. "The Passion of John Wojnowski," the headline read. "Haunted by his past, he has stood outside the Vatican embassy nearly every day for fourteen years. His lonely vigil has made him a hero to victims of sexual abuse. But will he ever find peace?"

I learned from the story that, at nearly seventy and five and a half feet tall, he worked as an ironworker for most of his life, building bridges and museums and nuclear power plants. Half a century ago, he said that a priest molested him in a small village in Italy when he was a young boy. He had never sought the help from victims' groups or filed a claim to the Italian diocese or brought a lawsuit. Instead, he stood on the sidewalk outside of the embassy with signs scrawled with statements like: "My life was ruined by a Catholic pedophile priest," or "Catholics Cowards," or "Vatican Hides Pedophiles." He told the magazine that he chose the location "not just because of its visibility—an average of 33,000 cars pass that stretch of Massachusetts Avenue each weekday—but also because he holds the Pope personally culpable for the church's failure to make him whole."

I printed the article out and put it on my desk in the Attorney General's office. I told my staff that we had to get in touch with him.

They found his son, and we arranged for John and me to get on a call. He knew about our investigation and the report, but he couldn't believe that for all those years, I drove past him and saw him there and made a mental note about what he was saying. I told him I just wanted him to know that I believe him and others believe him. I thanked him for standing out there. I thanked him for not quitting. I assured him that I wouldn't quit, either. He put a spotlight on this. I hope this brought him a little bit of peace.

CHAPTER IV

And Then I Walked into a Sheetz

THERE I WAS, ON A balcony overlooking the rolling hills of a resort in Mont-Tremblant, in Quebec. It was high summer, so the winding ski trails had turned bright emerald, draping down the tree-strewn mountains like crown jewels. Lori and our four kids were just within earshot, at the tail end of a five-day road trip around Canada in June 2019.

It may seem from these pages that my family and I take a lot of trips, but the reality is that because of work and our hectic lives it rarely happens. I don't think Lori and I have taken a real trip beyond a long weekend just the two of us since our honeymoon in St. Thomas in the nineties. It happens, though, that on the exceedingly rare occasions that we do plan to go away as a family, these trips, great and special as they are, have a way of falling in the middle of some of the most pivotal moments in my work life.

The picturesque, perfect-for-Instagram version of the trip was that we were all together in a resort town in Quebec with that gleaming sun shining down on those green trees in all their splendor, all the kids were on Cloud Nine, and I could just leave the weight of work at the office until I returned home.

The reality was slightly different. For starters, we had sky-high hopes that we had been geniuses to plan a vacation in the summer, when we would hike and hang out in this quaint town that would be free from high-season tourists.

When we got there, we realized that a big chunk of the town was essentially closed. As I recall, there was one open restaurant. Or maybe we had to keep going back to that same pizza place over and over again, because, of the limited options that were open, it's the only place our kids agreed to eat. And when we did go on a scenic hike we'd all been looking forward to, to which you had to take a ski lift up and down, Max, who was about ten at the time got motion sick. And he started complaining almost immediately that his neck hurt. Like the good parents that we are we kind of ignored him at first, then assumed he just was complaining because he didn't want to go on the hike. We then noticed tons and tons of very irritating little flies that were constantly swarming us in spite of the fact that we had all put on bug spray.

I looked at Lori and I whispered, "We can't win." But we kept going, trying to put on happy faces and ignore the bugs. Some of the kids put their shirts over their faces. Max kept swiping at his face and whining, and we were frustrated that the kids were not following our make-the-best-of-it plan. So we quit and went into the ski lodge at the top of the mountain to regroup.

Max had long, cool hair, and when Lori lifted up the back of his mop to look, his neck was bleeding everywhere, like it had been chewed on by a storm of mosquitos. He definitely had not complained enough. I, of course, felt awful, and we all promptly took the gondola back down and went right back to the condo to tend to Max.

"We've gotta get out of here," I told Lori. "I think we are done."

To top it off, I wasn't as able to escape what was going on back home as I'd thought. I was spending way too much time on that small balcony outside the room, on the phone negotiating, cajoling, coaxing an executive who came to be a symbol of what frustrated and angered people about the American health care system.

At this point, the executive, a guy named Jeffrey Romoff, had his feet to the fire. I just knew we were about to make the deal.

For the last two years, I had been in the middle of a dispute between UPMC and Highmark, two health care giants in the western part of Pennsylvania. The companies are behemoths. UPMC is the largest non-governmental employer in the Commonwealth. They operate under a vertically integrated system, where they are both insurance companies and medical care providers operating their own health care facilities and offering their own network of doctors. Highmark had traditionally only been an insurance company, until it acquired West Penn Allegheny Health Network, UPMC's closest rival. This put them in direct competition, meaning that they both then had their own captive doctors and their own hospitals. It wasn't long before UPMC attempted to stop accepting Highmark insurance from any of its patients who wanted to see doctors within its system.

The CEOs of each company—Romoff of UPMC and David Holmberg of Highmark—did not get along professionally. They hadn't for years. Romoff was notorious in Pittsburgh, and, fairly or not, was regarded as a stereotypical caricature of a CEO, someone who was making millions a year even though his company technically operated as a nonprofit. By contrast, Holmberg was a community oriented, kind man who operated without the brash bravado of Romoff.

Since 2014, the two health care giants had operated under a state-brokered consent decree that guaranteed that the most vulnerable patients, including children, the elderly, those in treatment for cancer, and economically disadvantaged Pennsylvanians, could continue to receive treatment from UPMC's extensive network of hospitals, doctors, and other medical providers.

That decree was set to expire in July 2019. Romoff vowed to make sure that anyone with Highmark insurance would no longer be able to receive care or see doctors at UPMC. This would have left hundreds of thousands of Pennsylvanians with Highmark insurance in a really tough spot. He was trying to put Highmark out of business and outwardly didn't show compassion for the people who'd be harmed in the process. Highmark, on the other hand, was not retaliating. It was still willing to see UPMC-insured patients and willing to agree to another deal. In effect, this meant that UPMC was coercing people to come over to their insurance plan if they wanted to continue to see their doctors, or if they wanted the flexibility to receive care from both. If we didn't come up with a solution, people would lose access to their doctors, prices would go up for patients and services would be more limited.

The problem was clear. There was only one bad actor, and there was a proven solution, because the companies were operating under an agreement that was, for the most part, working for people. But corporate greed corrupted. And so did a lack of political courage. Few of the local politicians wanted to take sides. This was a monumental deal in Pittsburgh, and all anyone could talk about, and yet very few people were doing anything about it. No one believed that Romoff would make a deal. He was waiting for the consent decree to expire to cripple his competitor. Many seemed resigned to UPMC just getting their way as they always did.

I wanted to prove them wrong, protect the people, and bring the two sides together.

Privately, we invited Highmark and UPMC to our office to talk about what could be done, what common ground we could find. Both sides postured and set up impossibilities to striking a deal. They would show up with huge, unwieldy teams of attorneys and communications teams. The lawyers would lawyer me and we'd have these long meetings and resolve nothing. This kind of BS—where everyone is seemingly paid to be unhelpful—is one of the things I despise most. Everyone wanted to tell me that they were right and every lawyer had something to say. Details of our conversation would end up leaked to the press and the whole thing was just an unproductive mess.

We were getting closer to the deadline, and I was getting more and more concerned about the impact on regular folks who were doing everything right but were about to get screwed. My team, led by Michelle and seasoned attorneys Jim Donahue and Mark Pacella, who had done battle with UPMC in the past, worked through scenario after scenario. But the normal way of doing things wasn't going to get Romoff to really come to the table. We knew that we had some moves at hand and levers we could pull. For one, because UPMC operates as a public, nonprofit charitable institution in Pennsylvania, it got tax benefits, donations, and public financing in exchange for a legal responsibility to perform services that benefit the public. Its nonprofit status saves UPMC millions of dollars every year—money that without that designation would be paid in property taxes to the city of Pittsburgh and Allegheny County, to finance things like education, infrastructure, policing, and a whole host of other public goods. Add to that the fact that for more than a decade between 2005 and

2017, the company got $1.27 billion in public and private grants to support its work.

That's a pretty good deal. But they had an obligation in order to hold up their end of the bargain, and part of that obligation included that they had to act in a way that was consistent with their charitable mission in all aspects of their business, including not making it difficult for patients who needed care to get it under their system. If they were going to take money that could have gone to Pennsylvanians by enjoying their perpetual tax-exempt status, they'd need to give back to those Pennsylvanians in the care they offered. At the very least, it meant offering care to all—including those with a rival's health insurance card.

Romoff and his board were hugely protective of their non-profit designation. We just so happened to have a very real case against them, because they appeared to be in violation of the Solicitation of Funds for Charitable Purposes Act, the Nonprofit Corporation Law of 1988, and the Unfair Trade Practices and Consumer Protection Law by letting our seniors and children and workers suffer because of corporate greed.

In February 2019, about four months before the deadline, we filed a seventy-three-page petition in court asking a judge to impose a modified consent decree that would continue the current working relationship between UPMC and Highmark. We argued that as a nonprofit, UPMC was required to provide affordable health care through negotiated contracts with any health plan. Excluding a major insurance carrier like Highmark was in violation of that. We added that UPMC had wasted charitable assets through exorbitant executive salaries and perquisites in the form of corporate jets and lavish office space. We knew that we had more lawsuits to come and cards to pull if they continued to not be willing to engage in real efforts to reach a new agreement.

It was at this point, in the thick of this negotiating standstill, when I stopped at a Sheetz to pick up lunch during a stop in the Pittsburgh area. Now, if you are unfamiliar with Sheetz—I am sorry that you are missing out on a national treasure—it's a twenty-four-hour gas station plus convenience store founded in Altoona that has a made-to-order kitchen from which you can order anything from pizza to "burgerz" to burritos to traditional sandwiches, really good coffee, milk shake machines, and a place to sit down and eat. The works. It's one of the Pennsylvania greats, and I can say that with authority, as someone who has traversed the Commonwealth and makes a habit of frequenting rest stops all over the place. Often, with an Uncrustable and a cup of coffee in hand.

That's what I was on my way to do that afternoon when the woman working behind the counter recognized me as she was ringing me up and said, "Can I ask you something?" Of course, I replied. "Can you please figure something out with this Highmark/UPMC thing? Because my husband has Highmark insurance through my work, but he's been getting his cancer treatments at UPMC. And if this isn't fixed, he's not going to be able to get those treatments come July."

I'd known this was going to happen to people all over western Pennsylvania. I'd spent months hearing about it, debating it, parsing through every detail. I knew the stats, that tens of thousands of customers who would find themselves out of network, hit with higher costs for UPMC services, or needing to find new doctors.

But hearing from that hardworking woman about how her husband, already going through what must have been the worst time in their lives, was going to have to find a new doctor, switch treatment courses, wait longer, and pay more to do all of it set me off.

All this unnecessary pain because a corporate health care executive was trying to put his competitor out of business and didn't seem to give a damn about the people who would be hurt along the way.

That's the exact kind of thing I can't stand.

*   *   *

I've seen this dozens of times throughout my time in public service, and I'd never been able to stomach it. Now, this is different from the Catholic Church investigation, for obvious reasons, but the principle is the same. These are decent folks who, time and again, get overlooked or taken advantage of because people in powerful positions don't seem to really care about them.

It boils my blood, as both a matter of principle and a matter of politics. We've become parties that are captive to corners of our society as opposed to protecting broad swaths. Too many have stopped treating people with respect, stopped listening and as a result, stopped serving effectively.

That's part of the reason I created a labor division in my office when I became Attorney General. I had seen too many workers have their rights violated and get held down by the system. I wanted a dedicated office to be there to take in complaints and really follow up on them, and if there were bigger system issues or problems, to bring them to my desk. I wasn't the first state AG to do this, but it has become more common since, for good reason.

I put Nancy Walker, a career labor lawyer, in charge of this.

One morning, in 2017, as we ran through our typical morning update, Nancy brought up that she had received a number of tips about issues with Glenn O. Hawbaker, Inc., and she thought we ought to look into it.

Hawbaker is a Pennsylvania-based construction company founded in the 1950s that works on every kind of infrastructure project—from highways to bridges, to providing aggregate and asphalt through a network of nineteen factories. In every state, the major contractors like Hawbaker are known entities, and for each infrastructure project, a state bids them out and gives the job out to the lowest bidder. Hawbaker did decent work, and was politically connected, and came in with the lowest bid for many jobs, so the state awarded them lots of work.

Our office started hearing reports from folks at Hawbaker about unfair labor practices. None of us had met any of the workers yet when Nancy first brought it to me, but you can imagine what that work looks like. It's backbreaking, dangerous work on the sides of highways and over narrow bridges. On a hot summer day, they would be the ones out on the roads doing the work.

We paired Nancy with a great criminal prosecutor Kirsten Heine and they got to work on an investigation into Hawbaker's labor practices. They uncovered that Hawbaker had been stealing from these workers' wages and retirement funds in a massive surreptitious fraud scheme. The way it went down was that if you worked for Hawbaker on one of these projects, you were owed at least a prevailing wage—a set, known rate that's agreed to at the time Hawbaker accepts a job. The prevailing wage includes health care and retirement benefits that ultimately get taken out of a worker's paycheck. If, for example, someone's prevailing wage is fifty dollars per hour, the employer might take ten dollars out of that for health care and retirement, so the worker would take home forty dollars per hour. When I was county commissioner, I passed a responsible contractor ordinance, which meant that construction companies had to meet certain standards, like setting up pension funds, offering health care benefits, training programs, and safety measures for all workers. So I was familiar with what these rights were, but I had never seen anything like this.

Hawbaker constantly bragged about its great employee benefits, but actually it was stealing its workers' retirement and health care money. Take our earlier example of fifty dollars an hour. They would lie and say they were taking five dollars per hour per paycheck for health care; it actually cost them three dollars. The company took the difference to line the pockets of Hawbaker execs. It was also stealing wages by using money intended for retirement funds to instead contribute to retirement accounts for all Hawbaker employees, including owners and executives. Then, because they were getting richer from stealing from their workers, they were able to offer lower and lower bids to the state, which would allow them to outbid everyone else and get more projects and screw over the honest bidders in the process. So for a road project that should cost $100 million, they would come in at $90 million, win the bid because they would make up the difference by stealing workers' pay. They'll pay the wages the same, so employees would not be suspecting, but at the same time, they were draining the retirement account and fraudulently charging more for health care.

Once I realized what we had here, I pushed hard and I told my staff that I wanted to meet the workers. I was introduced to one woman named Agnes Huber, who was a pipe layer for Hawbaker. For years, the job required her to mostly use shovels and hand tools, and as a result, both of her thumbs had slid off their bones by about a quarter inch. They didn't sit where they used to. They certainly didn't work the same. She told me about how hard she worked for the company, which was clear to see. The effects were right there shaking my hand.

"I can't imagine why they would have to take all this money from the people who were doing the work," she said.

Tim Lewis, a superintendent, was getting ready to retire after decades working daybreak till dark. He went to his accountant one day to get everything squared away before he officially hung up his boots. He'd blown out his knees from years on the job. His body just couldn't hold up. He'd put in this work, done his time, earned the rest. He gave the accountant his 401(k) statements and she couldn't believe her eyes. She told Tim that the money in his account couldn't possibly be all the money he had earned during his time working at Hawbaker.

"Tim, this is your 401(k)," the accountant said. "Where is your pension? What's here, this can't be it."

That's when he realized that something was terribly wrong. That wasn't dissimilar from Harry Ward, a semiretired bridge worker. It's a physical job, sure, but there was a tricky mental component to it, too, working on highways as drivers sped past.

"We sensed there was something going on because they would never give us straight answers," he said. He kept meticulous notes in a bound notebook after every shift, logging all the hours he worked so he knew he'd reached the number of hours he needed to retire. But he started to notice that the retirement statements he got from the company and the contribution amounts to his pension didn't match what was in his notebook.

By April 2021, relying on great team legal work with an assist from Harry's notebook, we charged Hawbaker with four criminal counts of theft relating to violations of the Pennsylvania Prevailing Wage Act and the federal Davis-Bacon Act. It was the largest prevailing wage theft criminal case on record in the United States. "My focus now is on holding Hawbaker accountable for breaking the law, and getting these workers their money back," I said in a press conference, at which workers stood behind me and shared their stories. Those were the stories that mattered. This case, like most for me, boiled up from the bottom—from the people who were wronged, whom I listened to.

That August, Hawbaker pled no contest and under the agreement with my office they were forced to make each and every one of these workers whole. I felt such relief, doing right by those workers. They are literally the people who build our communities. This was the least we could do.

Unsurprisingly, Hawbaker came after me in the press. I certainly hadn't made it easy for them. But I wasn't backing down.

Typically in these cases, as a condition of their plea, a company like this would pay a large fine to the state. In this instance, though, I wanted every worker to be compensated and paid what they were entitled to instead. And I wanted it to be done by Christmas, so they would have enough money in their pockets to buy their kids and their grandkids what they wanted for the holidays. Some on my team weren't optimistic Hawbaker would meet my Christmas deadline.

A week before Christmas, Hawbaker paid more than $20 million in stolen back wages to more than a thousand Pennsylvania workers. These were hardworking citizens trying to take care of their families. Once I heard their stories, once I put myself in their shoes and thought about what outcome I would want for me and my family, just as I had done with the woman I'd met behind the counter in the Sheetz, I was activated and motivated by them, for them. We wouldn't be deterred, held back by conventional wisdom. My team and I would fight for them. We would look for swift resolution. We would advocate and work as hard as we needed to in order to get the job done. We had to get them what they deserved, and we did.

* * *

The same anger I felt during my work on the Hawbaker case was what I had felt two years earlier, after my stop at Sheetz that day for lunch. I jumped in the truck and called back to my office and told them about the clerk at the counter."We are not going to fail at this. We can't have people not be able to get cancer treatments because some health insurance executive is trying to corner the market."

I told them that I was done with those formal meetings with way too many lawyers on their side of the table where we talked in circles and got nothing done. I want to meet directly with Romoff.

Romoff wasn't going to attend without counsel, they cautioned me. In fact, they said, he shouldn't. Fine, I told them. Then we're going to force his hand. We started hosting a series of public events and sharing stories with patients who were about to lose access to their doctors. We had Cheryl Sorek, a woman with breast cancer who had been going to the same doctor for a decade, who would no longer be able to see the team that'd become like family to her.

She was a September 11 first responder who was battling multiple illnesses, including undergoing a neck dissection to remove a tumor cutting off blood supply to her brain, as a result of her service. For years, she received her treatment at UPMC and was covered by Highmark insurance through her husband's work. But because of UPMC's unwillingness to treat the people most in need in order to serve its own bottom line, this American hero would lose access to her doctors and have to travel out of state to the Cleveland Clinic to receive specialized treatment.

With public pressure piling on, I called UPMC board members to let them know that I wasn't going to stop, that it would only get harder for them to ignore.

And then I called Romoff directly.

To Romoff's credit, he agreed to meet, one on one. He asked when and where. As soon as possible, I told him. He took UPMC's private jet to the airport in northeast Philadelphia. We found a cramped conference room there that had a window that barely opened. There was no food. The only thing they had were those tiny little plastic water bottles that each hold about three sips. We must have downed a dozen of them as we sat there that afternoon, talking for hours. Mostly, we didn't even talk health care that first day. I knew everything we had to hammer out, but I also wanted to better understand him—the man, not the caricature of a CEO. That hearing him out and listening to where he came from, how he grew up, what motivated him, how he wanted to lead his company would probably get me a lot further and give me better insight into why he was motivated to do what he was on the cusp of doing—knocking thousands off of their health care including the husband of the Sheetz lady.

At the end of the day, I told him that we should get together again the following day to really start working through this. He agreed.

I got home that night and Lori asked me if we had a deal. She knew how important this had become to me. She also knew that we were fast approaching our family vacation to Mont-Tremblant and Montreal, and that I would throw a wrench in our much-needed family downtime if we hadn't come to an agreement. No, I told her. "Well, did you at least work through the terms?" Again, no. But we did talk about life stuff, I explained. He told me where he grew up. What he liked and disliked. His views on politics. His personal life. Lori gave me a look that you might say questioned this approach, but she knows I am patient and I play the long game. She also knows my track record.

Romoff and I spent the better part of the next week intensely negotiating this. One on one. To his credit, he stayed at the table even when it was uncomfortable.

My stance was that UPMC had to take Highmark insurance at the end of this. But I also made it clear that I wasn't trying to bust his chops on the other parts of the deal. You can't screw people over, I said. Folks have to have fair access to health insurance. No matter which insurance card you carried, you had to be able to see your doctor. The rest of the details could be worked out.

A few days later, we left for our trip. I was on the phone with Romoff nonstop. The bugs made it so our hiking plans were not possible. All the family fun we thought we would have in this beautiful place was on the brink. Until Lori met a woman in the street who told her about Parc Omega, a drive-through wildlife park. The kids made it clear that they had absolutely less than zero interest.

Well, we told them, we have got to do something besides the skyline luge, which we must have done at least a hundred times already. So we got in our Toyota Sienna minivan, which was littered with spoiled half slurped GoGurts and snack remnants, and drove to this place in the middle of nowhere between Mont-Tremblant and Montreal, the kids complaining a good bit of the way. This plan reeked of desperation, as if we were in one of those Chevy Chase Vacation movies. Only difference for me was that Christie Brinkley was not talking to me in this scene, only Jeff Romoff.

We pulled up to Parc Omega and paid the entry fee, then we were told to buy these Costco-size bags of carrots to feed the animals. We didn't really know what to expect, but I started to wonder when I was reading the signs and the only actual rule for the place was: Don't feed the bison. We started to move the minivan forward at about 5 miles per hour. Soon, we had elk and bison and all sorts of animals coming up to our car and putting their heads in, drooling all over every nook and cranny of our already filthy van. Almost immediately, there was an attitude shift in the car. The whining was replaced by hysterical laughter. "This is the coolest thing ever!" they yelled. Everyone was in on it.

I didn't expect to find our family's unbridled joy in a filthy Sienna, with four kids, four hundred carrots, and elk slobber, but that's the thing about unbridled joy. It shows up in the places and in the moments when you least expect it.

It is worth noting amid all this happy talk that I cannot stress enough how disgusting it left our car, with these animals drooling all over the place and putting their heads in the car. So gross, in fact, that we decided to trade in our car and get a new lease as soon as we got back home rather than try to deal with it. But in that mess is where the fun lived. We never forgot it. It's one of those trips that has lived on in Shapiro family legend. I can still hear the kids' giggles and joyful screams when I think about that stop.

I think about that detour to the park a lot. How to just go with it. How we will always find the bright side together. How much I miss those days, crammed into the minivan, with all four kids giggling together at the same thing (or fighting with each other) in the backseat. How in the moment it forced us all to be, despite what I was balancing, despite the 10 year age span between the oldest and the youngest. How I'll never get that trip back, how even if we went back to that same park in the same car with the same snacks, it would never be the same again. I'm jealous of that dad, of that family, even though I am him and they are us. I'd give just about anything to relive it.

The final day of the Canadian adventure took us to Montreal, where we took a family tour of the city's downtown. Of course, the sky opened up to the most torrential rain we'd ever seen. I had no choice but to race to a street vendor who was wisely selling rain ponchos with Canadian flags on them. Soaked to the bone, decked out in the red and white, laughing until our cheeks hurt and our stomachs ached, we ate crepes (everyone loved) and poutine (nobody loved). We had an amazing dinner that night at Da Emma, a well-known subterranean Italian restaurant in a converted former women's prison in old Montreal. We headed home to Abington the next day laughing about how much fun we had on the worst trip we have ever taken.

Nearly the whole ride home, I was still on the phone about UPMC. These conversations were tense and tricky and complicated enough. There were two super entrenched sides debating a complex issue in which if you pulled at one string, the whole thing could fall apart. It was Jenga and Tetris with the highest possible stakes all at the same time. Now, add to the mix that I was driving a Toyota Sienna minivan in another country, full of elk slobber and carrot remains, where I had absolutely no idea where I was going. I had four young kids in the back who were being so good, on their best behavior, trying their absolute hardest to keep it down and let me focus, but they were still four kids in the backseat of a minivan for hours on end. My attention was in twelve places at once—on that phone call trying to hammer out the issue, with one ear to Lori trying to whisper the exit numbers to me as they crept up, another to one kid in the backseat who was quietly and politely asking for the Cheez-Its we had up front, and then promptly hearing those Cheez-Its not quite make it into his hands and spill out onto the floor around him—a mess I knew I'd have to try to vacuum up when we eventually got home. It's the realities of parenting on a road trip mixed with a high-wire act at work. All of it's a mess, and none of it I'd trade.

By the end of the trip, Romoff agreed to accept the terms of the deal. At the start, my lawyers had told me that if we could get him to agree to a two- or three-year extension of the consent degree, that would be a major victory. I told Romoff that I wanted it to be a ten-year deal, and that I wanted there to be only two signatories: Highmark and UPMC. I wanted to bring these two companies together—not use the long arm of government to force the relationship.

Romoff finally agreed. David Holmberg, the capable and compassionate CEO of Highmark, agreed, too—he was an easy sell. The three of us got on a call to confirm the deal. It was their first decent phone call in a long time. They agreed to work together to go from adversaries to allies in providing great health care to all who needed it.

I never would have gotten there had I not been motivated by the woman in Sheetz about the real impact that not winning this fight would have had on her family. And maybe Romoff never would have agreed without the public pressure. Perhaps he would have been less likely if the two of us hadn't sat down for hours and really talked.

When you're in these negotiations, when the disagreements seem insurmountable and divides so great, it's hard to remember that fundamentally, most people are pretty decent. Most want to do the right thing even though they feel constrained at times.

Moments like these are harder to come by in today's climate of political nihilism. Fewer people are willing to even have these conversations in the first place, let alone actually listen to what people who disagree with them are saying and let their minds open enough to be willing to maybe rethink where they stand. Or, at the very least, respectfully disagree. But I'm not willing to quit that hope. I still fundamentally, at my core, believe that we have more that unites us than divides. When we make space for these conversations, for relationships with people we don't always agree with despite the space between our views, good things can happen. Compromise is possible. It may not feel comfortable all the time. It'll take patience. But if we choose to look at each other with a good eye, to practice our faith in one another, to show up in these in-between spaces, we will, more often than not, find common ground.

To this day, more than half a decade later, people still come up to me with glistening eyes. They shake my hand and tell me that they got to stay with their doctors in Pittsburgh, or that they got their retirement money back from Hawbaker, or that they were a victim of abuse who shared their truth, got some accountability and felt that someone listened. That I'd fought for them and delivered.

I give them all a hug, tell them that I will keep doing that as long as I am serving them, which I hope is a really long time.

And then I get back to work, so I can keep doing just that.

CHAPTER V

"Is that something you would be willing to do?"

I WAS IN THE MIDST of a peaceful Saturday morning in October 2018. Mid paper, mid cup of coffee. It had only been two months since the Grand Jury Report about the widescale abuses within the Catholic Church had been released, so I felt like I was still on a quiet comedown from that whole summer. It was Shabbat morning, so three of our four kids were at home and present and in the protected little bubble that I'd been so desperate to climb back into a few months before.

Our daughter, Sophia, was out of the country for the semester on a class trip to Israel, and at that moment, was in Poland to visit Auschwitz. I was so proud that she was there, having that important experience. And as any parent knows, the pride gets mixed with a tinge of worry. So, of course, when my phone dinged, even though I was intent on a quiet morning, I immediately picked it up. It could have been Soph. I couldn't help but make sure.

It wasn't her, I saw immediately. It was a string of news alerts and messages from my staff, all coming at once. There had been a shooting at a synagogue in the Squirrel Hill neighborhood of

Pittsburgh. I turned on the TV and saw what everyone else was seeing at that moment—utter devastation, pure evil, as congregants who had gone to celebrate their faith in their community were brutally terrorized and killed by a right-wing extremist who had targeted them because of their faith.

The events were just unfolding, but it would later become clear that this was the deadliest act of antisemitism in the history of this nation.

Just before ten o'clock that morning, Robert Bowers entered the synagogue, which housed three congregations—Tree of Life, Dor Hadash, and New Light—through an unlocked door as Shabbat services got underway. Armed with an AR-15-style rifle and three Glock .357 handguns, he systematically made his way through the building, targeting worshippers who had gathered to pray and mark the Sabbath. Over the course of about twenty minutes, he shouted, "All Jews must die," as he carried out the attack. He had barricaded himself on the third floor by the time responding officers quickly entered the building. He injured two officers and two members of the SWAT team before he was taken into custody. He claimed the lives of eleven innocent worshippers that morning. They were community volunteers. Parents and grandparents. Veterans and doctors. They ranged from their early fifties to ninety-seven years old. They were all Jewish.

In the weeks and hours leading up to the heinous attacks, the killer had posted on Gab—a far-right social media platform—explicitly raging against a Jewish aid organization and referring to Jews as "invaders" in the US, making it clear that he believed Jews were orchestrating a plot to undermine white people. On the morning of the attack, he posted, "Screw your optics, I'm going in."

While this massacre would ultimately fall within the jurisdiction of federal authorities, in the initial hours, agents from my office were engaged in the investigation. I made arrangements to fly there right away.

I was reeling. I felt the pain of it, the sadness for the families and the state of the world. I knew that I had a responsibility as a dad, to make sure that I was there to answer all of my kids' questions about this tragic event while not having any answers of my own. This felt personal to us and our kids, that this happened in a synagogue and a tight knit Jewish community not unlike our own. I also wanted to be there for my team and for local law enforcement and for the families and with the community. I did not know what was needed or what would help or what I would do. But I knew that I needed to get there immediately. I had to be present. That was my responsibility.

I arrived at the scene, convened my team from the AG's office and met with local, state, and federal law enforcement officials to gather any information that I could before I went over to a Jewish community building nearby where the family members and loved ones of the victims were waiting. The FBI Special Agent in Charge brought me in the room as he tried to explain the inexplicable to the loved ones. He sat down at the table with them and I stood a bit off to the side. I wanted to make sure that, as they processed what had happened and talked to the FBI, their concerns, including the Jewish burial rituals were heard and articulated, though at that point, not even every victim had been identified. It was gut-wrenching, to be with a community that was so welcoming to me over the years experiencing such pain was just plain horror to witness.

"I can't wait to get home to you guys and just hug you," I remember telling Lori as I called her to check in. I really couldn't.

It was one of those days that makes you account for every exhale you can feel in your home, every finger you can count on your kids' hands, every hair on their heads. The voice of my wife coming through the end of my phone was enough and not enough at the same time.

"You will, but you need to be there," she said. Without question, I stayed.

We somberly walked across the street and packed into a church where the community set up a prayer service. Every last seat was full. People stood in the aisles. The Governor, Mayor, County Executive and scores of elected officials and community leaders were there. People from all faiths shared prayers, chanted songs, and observed moments of silence. The crowd just seemed stunned and also comforted by one another. After the service, we all filed out of the chapel and into the street. We stood at the intersection of Forbes and Murray, in the heart of Squirrel Hill. On any given day, this is a literal intersection of all faiths, where this church and Tree of Life and a Muslim mosque live in harmony. It's where, a week later, folks from that nearby mosque walked grieving Jews from the area to their Shabbat services to make sure that they felt safe, reminding us that no matter who you are or how you pray, we are one community.

It was a chilly fall night that evening at the intersection. Mist came down. In the face of what we now know to be one of the darkest days in our country's history, there we were, showing the power of coming together, different people from all walks of life, all different faiths, all different prayer leaders in the community, holding hands. I couldn't hear the words of those who offered prayers and blessings from where I stood, but it was just moving and beautiful and remarkable to be together, especially given the lack of humanity we had all witnessed earlier.

I spent the night in Pittsburgh and with the community—a synagogue and group of people so similar to the one I grew up in that it felt like home, they felt like my people, this felt like all of our loss. The next day, as the horror set in, prayer services were spontaneously happening all across the Commonwealth in all different places of worship. I spoke that next evening at an interfaith service at a synagogue in Philadelphia. "Hate speech begets hate crimes," I said. We prayed and cried and mourned together.

That week, I sat down for an interview with Jake Tapper on CNN. I'd known Jake forever. We went to high school together, though he is kind enough to mention that he is older than I am. His brother and I played on the basketball team together the year we won our conference championship. I knew where he came from and vice versa, so we both felt the weight of those few days on our communities and on ourselves. But we each had our respective jobs to do in that interview—he the journalist, me the AG. During the course of this emotional interview, he asked me if I thought the suspect should receive the death penalty, and without a beat, I answered that I believed he should. "I think that this is an appropriate case for the Feds to do that," I said.

I really meant it. When I ran for Attorney General in 2016, I would repeat the same line about my stance over and over—that I supported the death penalty for the most heinous crimes. It was pretty clear to me that what the murderer did in Pittsburgh that day fit that criteria.

My gut reaction to the question here didn't necessarily have to do with my faith. In fact, as a matter of Jewish law, capital punishment could be carried out, particularly for crimes like this. I wrote a paper about the Old Testament's perspective on the issue as a law student at Georgetown. The Bible laid out the very specific and serious circumstances that warranted the death penalty and the significant restrictions placed on capital punishment, like needing two witnesses to the crimes, prior warning, and knowledge of the potential penalty. My takeaway was that there was a higher level of scrutiny in biblical times to call for the death penalty than in our current justice system.

*   *   *

In the immediate aftermath of the mass shooting, the local community and the broader Jewish community across the country rallied around the victims and survivors. Vigils and prayer circles were held with people of all faiths. Prayers and donations and security and solidarity. The synagogue has been closed since the attack, but in 2021, the congregation launched an initiative to transform the site into a memorial and educational center, a place where people could pray and memorialize and actively learn about hatred, antisemitism, and the ability to rebuild from such despair. There would be a new sanctuary, along with a memorial to the victims, classrooms, a museum dedicated to learning about antisemitism and the Holocaust, and a center for interfaith dialogue and social justice.

I hold my relationship with the Tree of Life community dear. I draw a tremendous amount of inspiration and hope from them, as I have been fortunate enough to witness how they have been able to find light and peace amid so much darkness and carry on in the wake of such tragedy. I have particularly leaned on their steadfastness over the last couple of years, as I have witnessed the rise in antisemitism across this country. When I was sworn in as Governor, I recited my oath holding their Bibles. It's their menorah we light at the Governor's Residence to celebrate Hanukkah. There have been times when I have struggled to figure out what my responsibility is as a person so public about my faith, at a time when it is more tenuous than ever to be Jewish in America. In these moments, I look to the Tree of Life community as my guidepost for what it means to live our faith out loud, without fear or question.

This is definitely more true in a post–October 7 world, but I started feeling the swell of this when I ran for Governor. I'd have countless people from the Jewish community come up to me on the trail telling me how scary the world felt to them then, with the echoes of Charlottesville and the vitriol rising around the country during Trump's first term.

Of course, antisemitism has gotten impossible to ignore over the last few years—much scarier, much more real, both in the number of incidents and in how present it feels around us. I often have people come tell me they were comforted by the fact that I was willing to live my life openly and proudly as a Jew, that it gave them confidence to do the same. At President Jimmy Carter's funeral, for instance, I was sitting with my fellow governors, just behind the group of former presidents and first ladies, when a young man approached me. He was the grandson of someone who had worked for President Carter, and he wanted to tell me that how I lived my life, how proud I am of my faith, and how I practice and what I believe makes him more comfortable about being open about his faith and being proud of who he is. To hear that it's that impactful to others, particularly young people who take it in, made me think about it in ways that I had not before.

My faith has never been something I thought about doing a whole lot. Not because it's not important. The opposite, really. It's elemental. It's not something I check off a to-do list in the morning. It's just baked in to how I operate, to our family system and what I prioritize, to the why of what I do, and to the how of coming to decisions. Because of the nature of it, it's hard to put into words. It's why I sometimes sound a little vague when I get asked about my religion in interviews or when I try to put it into words. Kind of like when you get asked to explain how you fall asleep or blink. You just know to do it. It's part of you, without thinking. All essence and instinct. Now it is becoming clearer people are watching how I do it. They're understanding that piece of me just by witnessing it.

Unsurprisingly, I hear this sentiment from American Jews a lot. And I never heard it more than after the attack on my family and me at the Governor's Residence. The thing that they'd most commonly tell me was how scared they were. That if this could happen to me, then it could happen to any of them. But, they'd tell me, they saw how proud I was still. That I wasn't shying away from my religion, even in the face of the fear and the realities. That I was doubling down on my commitment to living my faith publicly. They were both fearful because it happened to me and comforted by how I reacted. But I also heard from people who aren't Jewish. In fact, a significant number of Christians and Muslims and people who don't consider themselves to be religious told me how sorry they were that this happened and that I shouldn't be deterred from openly practicing my religion. That it only emboldened their own commitment to their own teachings, or grounded them more in how they were raised. I felt held by their support, buoyed by it to continue. There is a shared, common humanity that I know binds us. Even when we disagree. Especially when we do, sometimes. That's what gives us strength.

I am in awe of how the Tree of Life community continues to be of their faith in the face of evil that has created such loss and such pain. It has only made me more proud to be Jewish, more willing and able to use my voice and whatever platform I do have in my position to speak out. It is a responsibility I take seriously, and the voices of those in the community continue to ground me.

It's because of that that I really do listen and take in what they have to say. A number of families in this community favored the death penalty for the killer. In fact, they represented many more. We talked it through at length. I heard them. It's something I still think about to this day. I honor and respect their feelings. And while I could never understand their pain, I am always trying to support them in any way I can and trying to see from where they sit.

At the same time, some in the community let me know that they were against seeking the death penalty. They explained that even after all the pain and anguish, they did not want the killer put to death. That he should spend the rest of his life in prison, they said, but the state should not take his life as punishment for him taking the lives of their loved ones. That moved me. That stayed with me.

I felt like, if they were able to accept that individual serving life in prison, then how could that not be enough for me?

*   *   *

When I had sat down with Jake Tapper for that interview in the raw days following the Tree of Life Massacre, I held my beliefs that the death penalty should be used in those extreme cases honestly.

It just so happened that, right around that time, I started to have to think about the issue less theoretically, as capital cases were coming across my desk and becoming more and more part of my responsibility as Attorney General.

A few things happened that sparked the evolution of my views on capital punishment, and they all seemed to happen concurrently. As Attorney General, I was seeing our criminal justice system up close for the first time as the chief law enforcement officer.

Two critical truths became abundantly clear to me about the capital sentencing system in our Commonwealth: the system is fallible, and the outcome is irreversible.

I enforced the law without fear or favor in my time as AG. I ran on this and I know that I lived that during my time in office. I pursued justice for every victim.

As cases involving the death penalty started to come across my desk as, often times old cases coming back after an appeal, it all felt much less black and white, far less certain than how I felt during that CNN interview.

The way the system typically works in Pennsylvania is that if someone gets convicted and sentenced to death, they can appeal to the appellate court first, then to the state Supreme Court, and then, ultimately, to the federal appeals court to see if they can make a claim there. Some defendants will ask for a hearing to argue that their lawyer was incompetent and they deserved a new trial. If a conviction is upheld throughout that whole process, and then a new piece of evidence comes to light or a witness has a change of heart, that could trigger a new appeal. Those old cases, long predating my time as AG, would come back to my office, and I would have to make a decision as to whether or not we wanted to go to court to fight to uphold the conviction, or if we wanted to allow the person to plead guilty to life in prison and take the death penalty off the table.

We would always consult the victims' families and others impacted in these cases. I never wanted them to feel unheard or that justice was not being served. I certainly did not want there to be any surprises. Most of the time, the victims wanted the death penalty to be withdrawn, especially if it meant an end to the endless cycle of appeals they had to endure. Not in every instance, though.

At the same time, I was also on the state board of pardons, which is comprised of five people: the Lieutenant Governor, the Attorney General, and three experts—one for victims, one for corrections, and one for health. We reviewed all pardons and clemency cases for the Governor. A simple majority vote could send a pardon case to him, but a unanimous vote was required for a clemency case. In case after case, you would see some questions about the convictions or whether or not the sentences were just outcomes. As I painstakingly reviewed these cases, my eyes were opened to the fact that the system was imperfect, that there was a lot of gray area. Putting someone to death is so final, that for the first time, I started to question if I really could be in favor of that kind of decision.

When it comes to the eleven lives taken from us at Tree of Life, the case was being prosecuted by the federal government who was seeking the death penalty. My office wasn't involved in the legal case but I paid careful attention. I was struck by how a few of the families who lost loved ones that day opposed the death penalty for the killer and how many others felt the opposite. They were torn, much like America is on this difficult topic. Their feelings, mixed with what I was witnessing in my official work in the AG's office, spun around in my head as I rethought where my heart was on the issue.

Ultimately, it came down to a conversation with my son Max, who was ten or eleven years old at the time. It was at the height of the pandemic, which meant I was Zooming into a lot of my work as the kids were Zooming into their school, all under the same roof. That day, I was in the middle of a zoom meeting of the board of pardons, which I took super seriously. My insides churned, because in every one of these cases, I knew I was recommending that someone would either die in prison or be released on clemency to go out in the community, where, if we got it wrong, could pose a risk to public safety. I also understood that freeing them would have its own ramifications for the victims and their loved ones. I felt an enormous sense of responsibility with every case I voted on. Of course, the Governor would have the ultimate say, but I was one of only five voices making these recommendations to him, so I obsessively read up on every fact of every case. I would be so emotionally spent leading up to these meetings that Lori would make a point to force me to take breaks throughout those days.

On one of her forced breaks, I walked out of the room where I took my Zoom meetings to find Max laying on the couch watching TV. He knew what I was up to in the other room and seemingly out of nowhere asked me if we had the death penalty in Pennsylvania.

I told him that other states had outlawed it, but that Pennsylvania still allowed it.

"But you're not for it, right?" he said. "Why is it okay to kill someone as a punishment for killing someone?"

I had no explanation. For him. For me. I couldn't even meet his eyes. I started to say the words that I'd said a bunch of times in the past to explain my viewpoint. "Well, in the most heinous of crimes—" I said, but I couldn't even finish. I felt like I wasn't being emotionally honest with my own kid. If I can't justify this to my son, to myself, then how could I be okay with the state putting someone to death for their crimes, no matter how heinous?

I toiled with the decision internally, though it was becoming more and more clear. By the time I launched my campaign for Governor in Pittsburgh on October 13, 2021, and began a multi-city bus tour, my inner conflict came to a head. At the very end of the tour the last stop our campaign bus pulled into was in New Castle, a rural town in the western part of the state along the Ohio border.

The first question I got asked during a stop at Pagley's Pasta, a neighborhood restaurant, in my first week as a candidate for Governor, was from a veteran local reporter from the *New Castle News*. The journalist asked for my position on the death penalty.

I can't say that I saw it coming. I can say that in my head and my heart, I knew what I believed. And though it was different from what I thought I believed before, what I'd talked about publicly, where the popular political line was on the issue, I answered honestly. I thought about Max. I said that my views had evolved. That over the course of a decade, I had asked myself whether death is a just and appropriate punishment for the state to inflict on its citizens. That I had painstakingly considered every aspect of Pennsylvania's capital sentencing system, reflected on my own conscience, and weighed the tremendous responsibilities I would have as Governor. If I were to win this election and take office, I would oppose the death penalty and not sign any execution warrants.

I would hardly be the first Governor to make this kind of decision. I wouldn't have even been the first in Pennsylvania to do so. I did hear, time and again, politicians call on lawmakers to reform the system—that it was flawed but fixable. I disagreed. I wanted to abolish the death penalty in Pennsylvania entirely. There's no fixing it, because I came to the conclusion that the state should not be in the business of putting people to death.

With renewed clarity, I had found what I believed was right, and I needed to be on that side of it.

I knew that there would be a lot of people who disagreed with me. I also understood that there are a lot of people out there who, whether or not they agreed with where I landed on this topic, would accuse me of changing my mind or flip-flopping.

In fact, if you look at polling, I am actually on the minority side of public opinion in Pennsylvania. I went the opposite way of what would be politically popular for me in the midst of this campaign for Governor.

But it was a matter of principle for me, not politics. It wasn't about playing a game or pleasing a constituency. It was about my conscience. About being able to look my kid in the eye.

There's no question that so much of politics over the last few years has become transactional, devoid of principle, rudderless. You don't need to look further than the handfuls of pardons doled out from the Oval Office to people who have done personal favors or publicly praised or were related to presidents.

There's plenty of justifiable criticism of these moves, and of politicians in general, for how wishy-washy and self-serving it can all seem.

And so it's understandable that when we see a politician change their mind, the initial reaction is, oh, they're just shifting their public views to match what's in the zeitgeist, to conform with the status quo of that micro news cycle. I get where that criticism comes from. That knock can be fair and true sometimes. But not always. For me, I want the people representing me to be constantly curious and thoughtful, to evolve. I want them to listen to people, to continue to grow from the responsibilities they face as they serve and to hear from those who challenge the way they think. I don't want them to be tied to old views just because they said they supported something in the past. I am proud of the fact that I listened to my conscience in the face of public opinion. I will always defend what I feel is right.

People have grown so frustrated with some of their elected leaders who just blow with the wind and take a poll instead of finding their pulse. I hear that from them a lot as I spend time in different communities. I try to stay true to what I believe is right regardless of what others think, even when that means changing my mind.

*   *   *

It was hard for me to fathom as county commissioner that I would be embroiled in a battle over what constituted love and commitment, but that is where I found myself in 2013. Since the mid-nineties, a Pennsylvania law defined marriage as a civil contract in which a man and a woman take each other as husband and wife. Same-sex marriages, even if they were entered into legally somewhere else, were void in the Commonwealth. Civil unions were also off the table.

This could not have been further from my personal beliefs. Love whom you want to love, marry whom you want to marry. I don't want you deciding that for me, and I don't want to be deciding that for you. These are choices to be celebrated individually, not limited by the government. Real freedom.

It was also clear that this was the direction the country was moving in, that more and more Americans were coming around to this way of thinking. But in many states across the country, still, same-sex couples were being stopped from marrying their partners under the law.

In July 2013, the American Civil Liberties Union filed a lawsuit on behalf of twenty-three Pennsylvanians who wanted to get married or have their out-of-state marriages recognized in the Commonwealth. The suit alleged that the state law refusing to allow lesbian and gay couples to marry violated their fundamental rights and the Equal Protection Clause under the Fourth Amendment. The suit followed the ACLU's Supreme Court victory in the *Windsor* case, which required federal recognition for same-sex couples who are married under state law. A year earlier, my friend Senator Bob Casey, who rose in the ranks as a conservative Democrat largely in the mold of his father who served as Governor of Pennsylvania in the late eighties into the early nineties, had come to believe that same-sex couples should be allowed to get married. The state Attorney General at the time said that she believed the Pennsylvania law was unconstitutional and that she would not defend it in court.

Internally, within my office in Montgomery County, there was a lot of support for the idea that we could and should issue same-sex marriage licenses to any couple that wanted one. It was the right position, one that would stand the test of time. Marriage licenses are issued by the Register of Wills in each county. In Montgomery County, the person who held that role was a happily married heterosexual man in his sixties named Bruce Hanes. He felt strongly that we should come out and issue marriage licenses should the circumstance arise. I made it clear I had his back and agreed with that principled stand.

At the end of July 2013, Ellen Toplin and Charlene Kurland who had been together for twenty-two years and were recently having a hard time with medical insurance because they were not legally married, walked into the Register of Wills office and asked for a marriage license. So did Tamara Davis and Nicola Cucinotta who had been engaged for more than a year, but until that day, their marriage license requests had been rejected.

The licenses were issued and I watched the couples exchange their vows and rings and shed a few tears as they went through the two ceremonies, which were filled with the kinds of joy and surety that all wedding days are. Perhaps with more reporters and county officials there than most. But still, plenty of love and warmth filled the air. The two couples hadn't met before that day. But now they were tied together, in history and in hope for couples like them to face fewer obstacles than they had.

The impact was swift. Hanes quickly issued marriage licenses for three dozen more same-sex couples, and the celebrations continued. But so did the outrage. Pennsylvania's health department, under the leadership of a conservative Republican Governor at the time, petitioned the Commonwealth Court to shut Hanes down, arguing that a county clerk had no authority to decide which laws to follow and which laws to ignore, which the judge agreed with. By mid-September, our county was banned from further issuing any licenses. We knew that we would carry on the fight and appeal it to Pennsylvania's Supreme Court. Our legal team, led by my able solicitor, Ray McGarry, had broken down all the ways in which our decision was backed up by the state's constitution. We felt sound in our arguments and buoyed by our beliefs.

Still, the backlash was swift, and it was personal. Montgomery County Reverend William Devlin issued a statement to me, saying that I should be embarrassed by the position I had taken based upon my religious traditions. "I call upon Commissioner J. Shapiro to meet with a group of pastors, imams, rabbis, and priests and say that you will join with us—that marriage is defined between a man and a woman," he wrote.

I took offense to this for many reasons, most of them obvious. And he was right that at the time most observant and Orthodox Jewish leaders were not in support of the right for same-sex couples to marry. If he thought that kind of public calling out was going to get me to change my position, then I don't think he has any sense of just how much my faith grounds me in my convictions. I issued a statement in response. "I'm not gonna be lectured by Pastor Bill or anyone else about my faith," I wrote. "If anyone would like a lesson in Judaism and their position on gay marriage, you can seek out Conservative rabbis that perform gay marriages, you can seek out Reform rabbis that perform gay marriages. I certainly am not going to be issued warnings and dictated to by the likes of Pastor Bill."

Soon after, a group of Conservative and Reform rabbis in Montgomery County backed me up. "We write as Conservative and Reform rabbis in Montgomery County in support of your position, and we hope that same-sex marriages will soon be legal both in the Commonwealth of Pennsylvania, and all over the United States," rabbis in the Old York Road Kehillah wrote in a letter. "While it is true some members of the Jewish community may not support same-sex marriage, the movements we represent believe that an evolving understanding of Jewish law and Jewish tradition both affirms this right and asks us as Jews to sanctify committed same-sex relationships."

A year later, in 2014, Pennsylvania officially overturned its law (for context, this was a year before the landmark Supreme Court ruling in *Obergefell v. Hodges*, which came down in the summer of 2015, and made same-sex marriage legal across the country). Montgomery County issued 174 marriage licenses in the first year, 118 of them to same-sex couples.

We had won. We didn't waver and bend to the opposition and

public pressure. I knew in my gut what I believed was right. I knew how to execute, had the courage of my convictions and stayed the course so I could actually deliver on what was the correct path.

*   *   *

That's the attitude I've carried with me throughout my career. I know what I believe, and I don't bend to current public sentiment or political pressure. I listen and I consider, but I don't bend. There's a difference. I keep an open mind, because my own views may evolve as my responsibilities or purviews change. But my principles are held honestly and tightly. They're just not going to be shaken by what's popular or in favor or by who shouts the loudest on social media.

That was particularly true in 2020, as the pandemic hit and the nation grappled with the death of George Floyd.

That summer was grueling for everyone, as our country was in the midst of lockdowns and protests. Tensions were among the highest I'd ever felt them, justifiably. There were mass protests across Pennsylvania and the country calling for states to defund the police. Immediately, I was getting asked left and right to choose a side. Did I support defunding the police, or was I on the side of law enforcement?

My views were nuanced at a time where people wanted a definitive Door A or B. In reality, I didn't think it was a binary choice. I fully supported law enforcement. I also believed there was a real need to reform the criminal justice system. There was a more balanced approach than all the heat on either side, one that I knew based on all the criminal justice work I'd done throughout my time as Attorney General and how close I'd grown to the brave and honorable law enforcement communities. I believed in being tough on crime and smart on reform. It was logical, I thought, but not popular at that moment in time.

Now, I mourned Floyd's death. I was pained watching the video of his murder, for the hurt of his family and his community and of Americans whose hearts and trust were broken. I wanted the cops who did this to him to be punished to the full extent of the law. That was not good policing. My heart broke, too. I was there for a gathering in my hometown, standing side by side with students, community leaders, and the local police. That's how it should be. There is a way to peacefully work together to address this crisis in confidence and call for change.

There are bad cops in this world. There are bad politicians. There are bad doctors and bad priests and bad teachers. They have real and harmful impacts on people and communities. They undermine trust in institutions. In my experience, those are by far the exception, and it was my responsibility as AG to make sure that the exceptions are handled and that there were systems in place to make sure they don't pervade.

I have spent a tremendous amount of time with law enforcement and first responders in my time in public service, though really it began long before that. My dad cared for a lot of kids whose parents were cops. It was something he sought out and prioritized as a pediatrician, because he knew what a sacrifice their work was. He wanted to serve their families as they did our family and community. I absorbed that and carried that through my time as state representative, where I became one of the go-to guys on matters involving law enforcement. I fostered that relationship with the police, because I genuinely respect them and the path of service they've chosen in life. What they do is incredibly difficult. It's dangerous. It's a job most people don't want to do. I got to hear about the kinds of problems they faced and were working through in their communities, and the kinds of problems those communities felt they had with police. They confided in me, as did the people pushing for systemic reform. So did frightened members in the community who wanted more constitutional policing in their neighborhoods. I listened to all sides and invested in what was lacking. As county commissioner, I heard from local police that their radios, many of which were bought in the late nineties, were being held together with rubber bands by the 2010s. The head of the local police association explained to me just how vital these radios were to his officers—that if he had to put one gun or one radio in one of his officers' hands, he'd put a radio—and that the current condition was near irresponsible. I knew we had to do something. We ended up getting enough new handheld radios and fourteen mobile devices to distribute to every police, fire, and EMS department in the county as part of our overhaul.

My ties to law enforcement and my window into their work broadened when I was elected Attorney General. This isn't the case in all states, but in Pennsylvania, the AG oversees not only the Commonwealth's lawyers, but also all of the investigatory agents—basically the US Attorney's office and the local FBI field office rolled up in one on the state level. I was constantly collaborating with them and with state and local police on our office's investigations. The relationship was central to my work—a real give and take—and one that I respected and needed and came to really value and rely on. I understood their work and saw how dedicated they were to the people they served up close and firsthand every day.

So when the calls for defunding the police grew louder, I'd spent enough time in communities all around Pennsylvania and with law enforcement to feel confident in my conviction that that was not the best path forward.

It was equally important to me to really think about how to reform the system. As commissioner, I oversaw prisons for Montgomery County, and that proximity to both how law enforcement polices crimes and to what prisoners face while incarcerated and after they're released guided my views on all of this. When I was commissioner, nearly half of the inmates in the county were on psychotropic medications to treat mental health issues or manage drug and alcohol-related issues. One of the first things I noticed was that, beyond the medication, we were doing very little to actually treat them and less to give them the skills they would need once they served their time and were released. My team and I broke down the major barriers to reentry, and we put a program in place that included more intensive drug and alcohol treatment, job training, parenting education, and anger management.

We noticed that access to housing was a pain point, as four out of five landlords screened out applicants who have served time. The same was true for employment, which was why we banned the box on hiring applications that asks if an applicant has a criminal record in Montgomery County. Access to health care and drug and alcohol treatment was also an issue. One of the things we learned was that instead of terminating someone's Medicaid when they were arrested or convicted, we needed to suspend it instead, because if a person was terminated from it, there was a three-month wait period to be put back on it, which could delay their access to treatment or care. But if we suspended their Medicaid instead, then there would be no delay. We also made a push to help prisoners get access to government documents they might need, like a driver's license and Social Security card, in order to get employment, housing, or medical care.

We were also one of a handful of counties nationwide to get a grant from the Obama administration to focus on reentry reforms. The result of all of this was that our recidivism rate dropped from over 60 percent to 17 percent within that control group. Reducing the recidivism rate has a ripple effect. It ensures the safety and security of the community, it protects taxpayers, and it improves the lives of returning citizens. That's just good sense.

As Attorney General, I chaired two committees as part of Pennsylvania's Justice Reinvestment Initiative II, a bipartisan effort aimed at reforming the state's criminal justice system to reduce incarceration costs, improve public safety, and lower recidivism rates. In 2016, as chairman of the Pennsylvania Commission on Crime and Delinquency, I was appointed chair of the Working Group, which was made up of representatives from all three branches of government and various criminal justice stakeholders. Over the span of a year and a half, we worked across the aisle to launch an extensive review of the state's criminal justice system designed to reduce ineffective corrections spending and invest those savings in proven public safety strategies by developing policy and legislative reforms.

These reforms sought to expedite the release of nonviolent offenders, enhance access to substance abuse treatment, and improve probation and parole support systems. In 2018, Governor Tom Wolf signed two of these bills into law, addressing issues like probation reform, sentencing guidelines, and post-trial rehabilitation. The bills were designed to save taxpayers' money and were aimed at releasing nonviolent offenders more quickly, getting prisoners into substance abuse treatment more readily, and providing more support for probation and parole programs that keep offenders on the straight and narrow once they return home. The adoption of the State Drug Treatment Program (SDTP)—a key outcome of our committee work—led to significant decreases in recidivism—a 10 percentage point drop in the one-year rate and a 12.8 percentage point decline in the three-year rate compared to 2017.

The ideas themselves were worthy, but they received a lot of praise at the time because they received bipartisan support. Common sense and kind-hearted government.

At the same time, when I took office, one of the top killers in Pennsylvania was heroin. About 12 Pennsylvanians died each day from these poisons that were far too available in our communities. In some places, we found that a packet of heroin was selling for less than a buck on the streets. Right away, we wanted to tackle this head-on. We arrested over eight thousand drug dealers during my time as AG and we were charging the higher level dealers with tougher crimes. If the drugs they sold resulted in someone dying, we tried to put them away for twenty to forty years. We were tough on crime, full stop. On the flip side, we were making it clear that once someone served their time, they would have access to the tools they needed so that they wouldn't end up right back there. We even tried to send non-violent dealers who were basically just users trying to feed their addiction, to treatment instead of prison.

When it came to Floyd's murder, I felt that two things could be true at the same time. I supported the peaceful calls for reform, and deeply felt all the hurt and pain. I also knew from my experience that if you really want to create safer communities for everyone, we need police. I heard that when I spoke to people in the neighborhoods, not just those walking through them as part of a protest. Now, of course, these police officers need to look like the communities that they're sworn to serve and protect. And they have to be properly trained and know how to de-escalate. When you actually talk to cops, many of them confided in me that they were not given the training they needed. Plus, I always felt we should invest in community organizations to do violence-prevention work. I believe that formula is the common sense, correct path forward and the right response to Floyd's death. Hire more cops, train them, reform the system, invest in the neighborhoods. Common sense. Some loud voices on the political Left came for me after I said all of that and challenged their assertion that defunding the police was the answer. Some even threatened to primary me and end my career. It's not a great feeling to have some in your own party coming for you. But I also wasn't going to say something I didn't believe to be popular on my own team or on Twitter.

After George Floyd's murder, my office pushed for a state-wide police misconduct database, which we launched in the summer of 2021. This required all law enforcement agencies to consult the database for information on disciplinary actions, performance evaluations, and attendance records as part of a background check. What this meant was that departments have access to misconduct and disciplinary records of officers that they're seeking to hire and all departments must participate, which hopefully gives the public more trust in the people who are there to protect them. We helped pushed this legislation through the Republican-controlled legislature, making us one of the first states with a divided government to take real action after George Floyd's murder.

My views were honestly held, though not easily condensed into a tweet. Like most things in life, there is nuance. Our law enforcement community runs toward danger and protects us when we are running from it. They, and the community they protect deserve constructive solutions even if its not the easiest political route to take.

The community knew I had their back and wanted to bring down crime and bring up the quality of policing. I think the police felt my genuine, honest support, and when I did launch my campaign for Governor two years later, I did so with the endorsement of the Fraternal Order of Police, a badge of honor I wear with immense pride, particularly as a Democrat.

On the trail, I pledged to boost funding for law enforcement and add two thousand state and local police officers, along with support for accountability measures that would ensure that the more police officers we hire, the more opportunities we have for them to get out of their patrol cars, walk the beat, and learn the names of the kids in the communities to create a level of humanity and cooperation between the police and the community that's going to help make us safer.

At the same time, I was also endorsed by criminal justice reform organizations. Because these groups felt my genuine, honest support of them and their beliefs, too. So much of the time, these groups are viewed dogmatically—that you're either for us or against us. It's possible to support our law enforcement community and want to reform our criminal justice system. You can want to address bias in policing through training and also commend the bravery of these people and the need for more of that in our communities. Follow what you believe is right, even if it's not popular, even if it's not conventional wisdom at the time. That doesn't mean those beliefs never change; there has to be a willingness to evolve, as the world changes, as your own particular vantage point and purview expands and shifts. Perspectives change, but core principles rarely do. Both sides will ultimately coalesce around what's right if they actually listen to each other and have the stomach for doing the hard work together.

*　　*　　*

The same was true during the pandemic in Pennsylvania. Governor Tom Wolf, who I know was making his best judgment with the limited information he had, held the position that businesses and schools needed to shut down and that masks be required in public in order to best keep people safe. He ordered roughly twenty-five thousand employees of Pennsylvania's prisons and care facilities to get vaccinated or take weekly tests for the virus. The policies were often challenged, particularly in a divided state like ours, where the Republican-controlled legislature fought all of this. As Attorney General, my office would defend Wolf's measures, as was our legal duty. In 2020, I argued that a judge's decision to block Governor Wolf shutting down non-life-sustaining businesses would cost lives. I also argued that mask mandates in schools would help protect children and families and prevent mass COVID outbreaks.

Personally, I would have handled the state's response differently. I didn't agree that all businesses should be shut down and that schools should close for extended periods of time. I wasn't shy about this when I was running for reelection as Attorney General. I also absolutely didn't buy into the conspiracy theories that my opponent spouted—that COVID was a "government-sponsored virus" and the death toll was inflated; that Governor Wolf's policy of readmitting COVID patients from hospitals to nursing homes caused thousands of deaths (obviously, this was untrue); that the vaccines, which he called "government's poison," cause autism and killed people.

I believe in science. I applauded the speed with which the vaccine was developed and distributed, and got the shot as soon as it became available to me. But my view is that we got the masking and vaccine mandates wrong. The better approach, I thought, was to educate people on the virus and on the measures they could take to protect themselves and those in their communities, and then empower them to make their own decisions. In my office, for example, I did not require that my employees get vaccinated or wear a mask. I told them that I was going to get vaccinated. I was going to wear a mask to protect myself and my family, as I was working around the state and meeting tons of folks and was just being cautious about getting sick. We ultimately had a 98 percent vaccination rate in the early days in my office, not because we forced anyone to, but because we talked about the benefits and left it up to them to decide what was best for them.

When I came out on the trail and said that I didn't think we got it right, but that we should learn from it and do it differently going forward, I was criticized by some folks especially some in my own party.

A few years later, it came up among party leaders. In the meetings I had leading up to Vice President Kamala Harris choosing her running mate for the 2024 presidential campaign, her team brought up my public comments in which I had been critical of how COVID had been handled at local, state, and federal levels.

I respectfully pushed back, asking if they believed that we had gotten everything right, to which they generally agreed that we had not. I just had been willing to say the quiet part out loud, even if it wasn't easy or popular or toeing the line to do so.

*   *   *

The reaction was similar when I ran for Governor as a tax cutting, permit reforming candidate. If you looked at the facts, it was too hard to do business in Pennsylvania. There were a number of factors that played into that. For starters, permitting took too long and I had a wonky plan to fix it. We needed more dollars available for economic development. And taxes on businesses, especially small businesses, were too high. In fact, Pennsylvania's taxes on business income were among the highest in the nation, certainly the highest among our neighboring states. Governor Wolf had signed legislation that would gradually reduce the corporate net income tax rate to close to 5 percent by 2031. That was a great start. I wanted to be even more aggressive. Because it should be easier to start a business here. The barriers to entry and costs to run businesses should be lower. It was just common sense to make it a friendlier place to start and own and run a business. Otherwise, we would—rightfully—lose out on these folks to our surrounding states whose doors were wide open for them. I wanted to be a pro-growth Governor who creates jobs and promotes economic opportunity, and in order to do that, it didn't matter if the policies that got us there were old-school Democrat or typical Republican.

In a similar way, I went against the grain when it came to energy production. My campaign for Governor was in its infancy—maybe a couple of weeks old—when I broke with Wolf on the centerpiece of his climate change initiative. The policy would impose a price on carbon dioxide emissions from power plants. There wasn't support from the Republican-led legislature, but it was under Wolf's executive authority as Governor to push it through. I just didn't agree with the whole policy. It involved joining a multi-state consortium, the Regional Greenhouse Gas Initiative, or RGGI. It was a progressive plan that he argued would have positive environmental and public health impacts.

I didn't like the idea of joining a consortium of entities across states, where money and business wouldn't necessarily flow back to Pennsylvanians, especially since we were the largest producer of energy among participating states. I was concerned we were giving up our competitive advantage, and that it would drive up electric prices for consumers. Every time I asked how this would actually make a meaningful difference in curtailing greenhouse gases, I wouldn't get a satisfactory explanation. I was also really concerned that it would make it harder for the building trades and others who worked in the natural gas industry to put food on the table for their families. I respect their way of life and believe we can support them and meet our climate goals. It's not an either or. It's a both and.

I wasn't being contrary for the sake of it or trying to stand out from the pack. This was just what I believed. I wanted to help build consensus around an idea that I thought best served my state and help bring leadership to where that was, I told Pennsylvanians as I asked them for their votes.

*   *   *

I knew this to be true about myself. It was never theoretical, that I was willing to make a choice and then execute it. I'd been living that out for as long as I could remember. I'd been willing to pay whatever political price, if there was one, though truthfully, what usually happened was that I was able to lead people to where I was or at least lead them more in my direction. But a lot of the time, those things happened on my turf, under my domain. It's a whole other thing to make those gut calls and then stick with them on the world's stage, with the external and internal pressures turned up to an eleven. When all eyes were watching. When every voice had something to say. When the stakes could not have been higher. It was a true test of this as I sat down with Vice President Harris's team in the summer of 2024 as part of their VP vetting process during their newly formed presidential campaign.

It wasn't exactly a secret. Chatter about whether or not President Biden would stay in the race, or if he should stay in, started well before the summer of 2024, when he officially dropped out. When Lori and I attended the Japanese state dinner at the White House in April, more people than you would have imagined *within the Biden administration* were whispering about it, which blew both of our minds. His own staff was asking how bad it was on the ground in the most crucial battleground state in the country.

I know Joe Biden. I've known him since I was a pre-teen lobbying on behalf of my pen pal Avi Goldstein and the Soviet refuseniks. He is a good man, an honorable person. He has dedicated his life to service in a way I greatly admire. Our personal relationship is deep and meaningful to me, and our working relationship has been fruitful and real, particularly once I became Governor. I'd ride along with him in the Beast when he made stops in Pennsylvania, and he'd hear me out on what I needed from his administration to better serve the Commonwealth, what my take was on how people felt about him and about Trump. I wasn't going to talk behind his back, just because some others were.

I saw bad poll after bad poll but it didn't take a poll to confirm what I felt on the ground, the President was down and falling. I was honest with his team about that. I didn't know their internal process or which way their deliberations were leaning. But I knew he was in real trouble in Pennsylvania.

I saw what most people were seeing, which became harder to ignore after Biden's debate performance. There were a few schools of thought: Some people thought that even with that disaster of a performance, Biden still had the best shot at beating Trump since he was the only person to do it up to that point; others felt that there needed to be a process by which the party would handle this and nominate a replacement.

Privately, I was starting to feel real doubt about how Biden would win. And I certainly didn't think that anyone would be able to leapfrog over a sitting Vice President to accept a nomination at that point in the race.

I just wanted the strongest nominee with the best chance of winning, because the stakes were so high. Besides, I had a state budget to pass that weekend. I was working insane hours. That was my job and that was my focus. I didn't have much additional capacity to worry about something that I couldn't control.

That weekend, in July 2024, Biden and the First Lady were coming to do a rally in Harrisburg, which their team asked me to join. I was so wrapped up in the budget and really couldn't justify leaving the negotiating table to do some campaigning. At the last minute, the President's team asked if I could meet them for coffee. The three of us—the President, Jill, and I—sat down at Denim, a local coffee shop across the street from the Capitol. After the photo op and ordering our drinks, we pushed some stools together and had a private moment to talk. He asked how he was faring in Pennsylvania. I was honest with him. I told him that there were a lot of people who thought it was best for him to get out of the race. I shared some of our internal polling with him and my feel from being out in the community, and he told us his team had different numbers that showed the race much closer. He said he still had confidence that it would be OK. I shared that I felt he had the burden of responsibility to show folks here that the debate was an aberration, that he could turn it around and had a plan to address concerns about both his capabilities and voters' chief concern: rising costs. He acknowledged that and explained they had a plan to get him back out there as we sat along the counter facing the window overlooking the Capitol. We talked for about ten minutes before his team and the First Lady signaled it was time for them to head out. I walked him out to the Beast, shook hands, and wished him well. It was respectful and cordial, given the direct nature and candor of our conversation. He gave me no indication that he would be dropping out days later. I called Lori after the meeting and she asked how it went. I told her I was honest with him and that it seemed to me he was in it for the long haul.

The following weekend, I did a campaign stop at Reading Terminal Market with Vice President Harris. We walked through the large urban market, picked up the food her staff pre-ordered for her, did a quick press gaggle, and headed back out. This whole thing took about twenty minutes.

It was good to see Kamala; we'd been friendly for the past twenty years and were both former AGs. It was also good that it was a quick stop, since I was desperate to get back to my family for a quiet weekend after the budget storm and the grind of everything else.

Just us. I promised.

By about four o'clock, as I got into the truck to head home to Abington after leaving the VP, I imagined how we'd spend our night. You never know with teenagers, but I hoped they'd be up to doing something, anything together. I walked in the door and randomly they asked if we could try pickleball together at the court our neighbors had put in up the street. We'd talked about playing a bunch of times before but it never happened. I also wasn't sure I wanted to buy into all the hype. To my delight, Max and Reuben were as excited as I was to spend time together. It was July 13 and it was warm out.

"Nice shot!" I yelled across the court as my boys whacked the ball. We'd hit the ball barely twenty times before a message popped on my Apple Watch from Dana, my right hand, saying that former President Donald Trump had been shot. It took me a moment to gather myself. I prayed for his safety and the safety of everyone else who was at that rally in Butler, Pennsylvania.

I left Lori and the boys to finish playing with our neighbor, Larry, and I raced back home to coordinate the response with federal authorities.

Within an hour, we knew Trump was thankfully not seriously injured, but we had concern for the rally attendees. There was, of course, a mixture of extreme relief, and, quite honestly, a re-sounding fear. The people in Butler, a wonderful rural commu-nity in western Pennsylvania, were rightly terrified. Americans, even those who didn't support Donald Trump, were in shock. The political violence and what it meant for the state of our dis-course and future of our country weighed heavily.

President Biden called me twice that evening. The first time, he was checking in to see what I knew from my team on the ground and to share what he had gathered from the White House. The second time, he let me know that he had spoken to Trump and told him there was no place for political violence in this race. We lamented the rise in political tensions and had a very personal conversation about how he was doing post debate, acknowledging that he felt like people in the party were abandoning him. He reiterated that he wasn't going anywhere and that he appreciated my candor. The polls aren't that bad, he told me. We're going to be okay. Seven days after that call, he dropped out of the race.

I traveled to Butler the next morning. By then, we knew that we had lost one Pennsylvanian, Corey Comperatore, a fifty-year-old firefighter and big-time Trump supporter. Corey was killed by a bullet meant for Trump. Two other people were critically injured. I'd been to the site of the rally before that morning, but I asked to be taken there to survey the site for myself.

I then made my way into a conference room at a nearby township building to prepare remarks. As I sat there, I couldn't get something Lori had said earlier that morning out of my head. She'd told me that I wasn't there just to talk about Trump or about politics. I was there to speak about the people who had just gone to what they thought would be a typical political rally and left the victims of violence. Those people, their pain, they were my focus. They were the people I needed to show up for. I wanted to make sure that I reached out to them.

I knew enough to know that Trump rally goers were not preternaturally inclined to receive my call and words of support. But this was deeper than politics and I wanted them to know I gave a damn about their families, not just the impact this has on the former President. I left a message for one of the families of the injured and never heard back. I had a very short, polite conversation with the other. I saved the call to Corey Comperatore's wife, Helen, for last. She asked if I could wait fifteen minutes so her adult daughters could join, too. I didn't know this at the time, but she had refused to take President Biden's call.

I'd had to make these kinds of calls before over the course of my career and my time as AG. They start off slow; grief is often terse. Sometimes people open up and want to talk, and other times, the calls are brief and I think they're just grateful that I cared to call and honor their loved one. I follow their lead. In this case, after expressing my sorrow for their loss and telling them that Lori and I were praying for their family, I asked Helen if she could just tell me about her husband Corey. I'd learned a little about him as the news broke, and he sounded like a good man. The kind of quality people you meet throughout Pennsylvania. Helen cracked right open. She couldn't help but talk to me about how much he loved his community, how he went to church every week, volunteered at the fire company. His daughters intermittently jumped in with a story. Taking it all in, I said, "So, he was a really good girl dad," which mercifully made them all kind of chuckle.

Helen then said, "He dove on us to save our lives from the gunfire." I told them that in the depths of their grief, they could know that their husband and father was a hero, and how extraordinary it must feel to know that a hero had loved them. I told them about my faith and how much strength it has brought to me in my life, and that while we didn't share the same faith, I knew theirs would bring them calm. They shared about their own beliefs and practices and how they could lean on their community, as I do on mine. Before we hung up, I told them how much I appreciated that they were willing to talk to me and to hear me, and that I wouldn't share that we talked or what we talked about, sensitive to the notion that maybe they'd prefer it to be private.

"No," Helen said. "Share it with the public. I hope you tell people. I want people to know that Corey died a hero."

A few minutes later, I carried an index card with my scribbled notes from our conversation out to make my remarks. I started off by saying that the assassination attempt on the former President was absolutely unacceptable and tragic, and that Lori and I were grateful he was safe. I talked about the three Pennsylvanians who had been shot, and then I turned my attention to Corey. He was a girl dad, I noted, a firefighter who went to church every Sunday, who loved his community, and most especially loved his family. I looked at the cameras and told them that Corey died a hero. That Corey was the very best of us. That his memory would be a blessing, a phrase central to the Jewish faith in times of grief and loss. That night, I added, had shocked our community, our Commonwealth, and our country, and political disagreements can never, ever be addressed with violence. This was a moment when all leaders needed to speak and act with moral clarity, where all leaders had the responsibility to rise above hateful rhetoric and search for a better, brighter future for our country. I asked for everyone to pray for the two Pennsylvanians who were still in critical condition, for our former President to have a speedy recovery, and for the Comperatores, who would have an empty seat at their dinner table. We needed to make sure Corey's memory would forever be a blessing, I said, and here in Pennsylvania, I assured them that would be the case.

I walked back inside, still thinking about Helen and her daughters. Over the course of that evening, my phone exploded with messages from people from all walks of life letting me know that my remarks had struck a chord. That I had represented those families well and had done right—not simply as some politician speaking after a politically charged tragic event, but as a leader who understood how to show up for the families I represent. I went home to Lori and the kids that night, reflecting on so much—the family without their dad and husband, our community in shock, the rise in political violence—including what this all might mean for the stakes in the upcoming election.

About a week later, just before President Biden announced that he would not seek another term, I was in Bucks County, which is all the way across the state, when a cop stopped me at an event. He told me how meaningful my comments about Corey Comperatore had been, and that he couldn't believe a Democrat who supports Biden and Harris would ever speak so warmly about a Trump rally attendee.

How did we as a nation get to a point where people are surprised to see their leaders show up when they are needed most? Where it's politically risky to show up for everyone, to listen to and respect and support people you agree with the same way you would with those you don't. Like we need to pass a series of political tests in order to associate with each other. When did people start to believe that you are only there to represent the people who voted for you? That we should shut out the opinions we don't agree with rather than debate the ideas. Fear mongering and demonizing has replaced compassion in our political climate.

I know that it's when we stop listening that we cut off connection. And without that connection, our ability to empathize evaporates and our compassion vanishes. You stop seeing those you disagree with as people and neighbors and Americans and start viewing them as enemies. It's a corrosive cycle, and as a result, we have lost belief in each other—and belief, period.

When this cop said this that day, I immediately thought back to a couple of years earlier, when I was running for Governor. At the time, the largest donor to my opponent, Doug Mastriano, was Jim Martin, the executive chairman and son of the founders of Martin's Famous Pastry Shoppe. For those unfortunately uninitiated, Martin's is a Pennsylvania-based bakery best known for its potato rolls—a standout roll that truly deserves the recognition it gets.

Mastriano was not just my opponent. He is an election denier who was subpoenaed by the January 6 committee and an extremist who earned that moniker. He walled himself off from people who didn't talk like him, worship like him, marry like him. Folks in Pennsylvania were so concerned about him that they were willing to take off their red jerseys and their blue jerseys to come together and defeat someone like him. It had been a long time since I'd seen that kind of unity.

Campaign finance filings are public, and Mastriano's campaign had very little money. So his largest contribution, which was in the six-figure range, stood out starkly, and it came from Martin. Pennsylvanians were upset by the donation and his support of a campaign like Mastriano's, so they started boycotting restaurants that served the rolls and stopped buying them at the supermarket. One of them was Shake Shack, which used Martin's potato rolls as buns for its burgers. The whole movement started to get some legs.

When I got asked about whether I supported the boycott in an interview around that time, I knew most people expected that I'd say yes and pile on. The company was my opponent's biggest supporter. The boycott was gaining momentum. I was perfectly clear in my response: Martin's was a great Pennsylvania company, and more than anything, I thought Martin's makes a damn good roll. I was not for boycotting a business in our Commonwealth that employs hundreds of my neighbors. The Martin family, I added, runs a private company and has a right to support and employ whomever they want. I believe every company should make the decisions they think best for them and their customers. Boycott basically over.

About a week later, I got a letter signed by a number of Martin's employees thanking me for what I said and wishing me the best in the campaign.

Years later, when reporters asked Martin's President Tony Martin about working together despite our political differences, he could not have been kinder. "I would say it's a partnership, and he's leading Pennsylvania on the executive side and done a great job of cutting red tape. We may not agree on everything, but we agree on business, and we agree on helping Pennsylvania."

I thought about those Martin employees and that cop who came up to me in Bucks County and shared he'd been so surprised at my words in Butler. I let it play over and over again as the race started revving up around me. We had gotten to a place where there was such surprise over the fact that an elected official would reach across the aisle and try to do the right thing in these moments. That I would try to represent everybody. That this was just what we have come to expect of a politician. That we've all just accepted that.

*   *   *

That stayed with me the rest of that week, which was otherwise a blur of handling the fallout from the assassination attempt, the Biden chatter, my other responsibilities.

By the following weekend, Lori took the younger kids on a spur-of-the-moment trip to Vancouver, Canada, to visit my sister, her husband Jon, and their kids, who were spending time there while Jon filmed a TV show.

I hung out alone at the Governor's Residence with the dogs until that Sunday, when Jonah came to Harrisburg to spend the weekend with me. His friend's family had dropped him off, so

I was giving them a tour when Dana called me to tell me that Biden had just tweeted that he was dropping out of the race. I quickly excused myself as a tour guide and went out to the porch, where I sat with Jonah for the rest of the day.

Well, now what? Maybe there would be a process the party would engage in to replace him? Did I want to be part of that?

I tried calling Lori, who was out of reach in a Walmart in Vancouver. Dana, who had been enjoying a proper weekend at her friends' pool, got to the Residence, and we sat outside on the porch with Jonah, trying to manage the incoming.

Finally, Lori called me back. Nothing says power player like competing for my wife's attention with a superstore.

"I am in a Canadian Walmart right now. Maybe not the ideal time for this conversation," she said, "I don't think we are ready to do this. It's not the right time for our family. And it's not on our terms."

I agreed with her, on all points. But I also was aware that you don't exactly get to set your watch. Sometimes your watch is set for you. We never went down that road and I quickly made the decision that the best thing for us, for the country, was to endorse Kamala Harris and help quickly unite our party behind her candidacy with the hopes of making up the ground that Biden lost and give us a shot to defeat Trump.

Within a few minutes, Biden tweeted a second time endorsing Vice President Harris.

Minutes later, I got a call from Jaime Harrison, the chair of the Democratic National Committee, a good man who was making calls to explore where various leaders would be on a potential nomination fight. I knew full well that I did not believe that process was going to go anywhere and that I had already made up my mind.

I missed a call from Kamala ten minutes later. I didn't have the number she was calling from in my phone and my line was ringing off the hook. Her team tried reaching me through Dana, and we got connected a few minutes later.

She asked me for my support, which I offered immediately, and if I would put out a tweet or a statement saying that I was for her in order to build momentum. Of course, I agreed.

We drafted a personal and thoughtful statement and sent it out within the hour as my phone continued ringing nonstop. While all this was going on, Jonah stepped away from the table to call Lori.

"I've learned more sitting here with Dad over the last few hours than in all my years in school," he said. "I can't believe this is how all of this works."

Having him there in those moments, watching him soak it all in like a sponge, was the high point of the day. I'm far from a perfect dad. For every story I've shared in these pages about having missed a family dinner, there are dozens more that I haven't talked about. They'd bore you and you get the point. And I love public service. Every single day, I am grateful that I get to wake up and do it. There's nothing in this world I'd rather do. I know how fortunate I am to be here, and I've worked so hard to get to this place. I also know that I am here in service of the people of Pennsylvania, and that work fills me with such great purpose. It's my goal and my duty and my honor to put in the work and to give them my full time and attention. I wouldn't do it any differently.

And yet as I feel that gratitude and honor and call every day to show up for them, if I am being fully honest, I relentlessly struggle with whether or not I am being the dad I want to be because of the demands of the work I have chosen. I try my hardest to be at as many games as I can, home for every Shabbat dinner, driving the car on every road trip. Because I want to be. My heart is there. Of course, I ask myself whether the people of Pennsylvania will think I'm slacking on the job if I take time off to have quality time with my family, as irrational as that thought may be. But the thing that I toss over and over in my mind more than anything is how all of this will be remembered and internalized by my kids. Will they remember me as a present dad who tried to show up for every moment I could, or are they going to think of the times when I didn't get home in time? Will they think of me as the dad who crammed in twenty minutes that I didn't quite have in my day to have the catch? Will they know I was at the game on the sidelines, or see that I was there on my phone as I watched them? There are a million invisible calculations like this that every parent makes. And the only tally that matters to me—the one I pray for the most—is that my kids know that always, they were who mattered.

I tell myself that you have to be present where you are. When I am at work, I am at work. That's where my head is. And, hard as it is with the nature of what I do, I try to be as present and in the moment with my kids as I can when I am with them, too. And it can be a challenge to just listen to what they're going through. I'm a fixer by nature and nurture, because of how I grew up and the realities of my job. Those instincts are really hard to turn off. We all know that sometimes kids just want a shoulder, not a solution. And I know that our life is rich and full in the ways that matter, that will hopefully shape them into the human beings we know they can be. All of it has to do with modeling what it means to be a good spouse, a good parent, a steward of our faith, a listener and doer, a citizen and friend, a leader and person who shows up. I am proud of the fact that my kids get to see their dad in the arena and grappling with hard things, trying to do what is right.

*   *   *

Within just a few hours, every cable news outlet and person on social media had moved on from the news that Biden was stepping down. They now focused on how Kamala all but locked up the nomination and on speculation about whom Kamala might choose as her running mate. Suddenly, my photo was all over the screen and my name was getting bandied about. It was hard enough for me to get my head around. I can't even imagine how strange that must have been for Jonah as we sat there on the porch together fielding calls and watching the news.

Some seventy-two hours later, I was sitting in my office in the Capitol when I felt my phone buzz. It was Jen O'Malley Dillon, Kamala's campaign manager.

"The Vice President asked me to call you," she said. "She would like to vet you for the position of Vice President of the United States. Is that something you would be willing to do?"

CHAPTER VI

99 Problems

YES, I TOLD HER.

With my phone to my ear, I walked over to the corner of my office, where the first official map commissioned by the state House and presented to the first Governor of Pennsylvania, Thomas Mifflin, hangs on the wall.

I couldn't help but choke up.

I've never really cared about accolades or awards. That sort of stuff just doesn't do it for me. It's nice, but as I'm someone who grades against myself, it's never really been a motivator. But this moment meant something. It carried weight. It felt real. It was a reflection point.

I busted my tail to get here. Lori and I worked hard to build this life. Our kids sacrificed so much. And I felt very, very proud of what we had accomplished. We grew something. Whether or not I would get picked or if I even wanted to be picked, I was one of a handful of people being seriously considered for the second highest office in the country. It would be hard not to feel emotional about that.

I tried calling Lori. No answer. That's about right, I thought. Why start answering now?

I knew she wasn't ghosting me, she was tied up with the kids, but I also sensed that she sensed something was up that maybe she wasn't ready to deal with just yet. She called back a half hour later.

She was appreciative of the moment and totally honored by the fact that I was being considered, and, at the same time, full of trepidation. I couldn't help but feel it, too. I knew that despite the honor of it, it just didn't feel right for some reason. A push and a pull that I sensed would only get stronger which would make it harder to feel my truth if I continued down this road.

We'd been through campaigns before. But this was a whole new level of scrutiny, and a point at which I would have to do a lot of soul searching about whether I would even want the job.

And that soul searching would have to happen, like, yesterday, because the process started to move immediately, at a turbocharged superspeed. Dana Remus—who was White House counsel in the Biden administration and would co-lead this process for the VP—ran us through the process, including the zillion documents that we would have to gather and the few hundred questions we would have to answer. Within a day or so, we got on Zoom sessions with attorneys from the law firm whose job it was to go through all of the answers and paperwork. It started with financial questions, which was very quick for us, because Lori spent the last twenty-two years raising our children and serving our community, and the only money I have ever made is publicly disclosed and filed every year with the state. We don't have any controversial investments or assets. I am certain that this part of the process is burdensome for some, but it was the part we breezed through.

I did, however, have to comb through boxes we have piled up in our attic to try to find the years of tax returns they needed to vet me. We were in the midst of all these meetings and questioning, and there I was, in sweats, on my hands and knees, papers strewn all around me, looking for the few pages they needed. Of course, I handily located a copy of our original mortgage. I found the first car lease we'd ever signed no problem. I could find every single bit of useless paperwork I had no reason to hang on to with ease, but the few pages of tax returns they actually needed from me? Nowhere to be found.

I didn't hear Lori's footsteps coming into the attic, but she saw me there, on all fours, piles of useless paper around me, in all this glory.

"This is who they may want to help run the country?" she said. We laughed hysterically. It was a break for us, a moment of light that we very much needed.

The meetings with the lawyers went on for about a week, for hours at a time. Because there really wasn't anything there, and because I had been vetted so many times in elections before, we moved very quickly away from the questions that have ended other campaigns and into territory on positions I had taken that were against the typical grain. They were focused on the areas on which Kamala and I differed, like energy, cutting taxes, supporting law enforcement, and of how I thought COVID was handled. On the latter, they brought up an ad our team made in which I had said I thought it was clear that no one got it right, and that it was important for leaders to learn from that moment. I told them that it didn't seem all that controversial to me. I believed that when I said it, and I believe it still today. It became clear that the people vetting me viewed that as something that could be used against Kamala, that I was somehow criticizing her.

I wasn't being critical of her, I told them. But I didn't think that the Biden-Harris administration got everything right. Nor did I think that the Trump administration did. No one did, and we all have to learn from our mistakes. That's good leadership. That's a good way to live in general.

They moved on to a series of questions about my stance on police, and all of the questioning felt unnecessarily contentious. There were questions about why I was vocal about the need for more law enforcement at a time when that certainly wasn't popular or the conventional wisdom. I tensed, shifting in my chair.

Look, I told them, we need to win the swing states—especially Pennsylvania—and the reason I have earned the support I have from Pennsylvanians is because I have at times been willing to take different positions because they're what I believe. Because I reflect the common-sense sensibilities of my home state. My support on these issues from people on both sides of the aisle is a huge part of the reason I am here. I have won every election I have ever run for with the exception of that high school race in the swing state that mattered most to them—and perhaps to the election. And I am happy to be here, and honored, and this is the process, which I am fully submitting to, and they have every right to ask anything, probe everything, cross every T and dot every I. I respect that. I understand that. I know that's the whole point of this. But, with total respect and understanding, I'm not going to apologize for who I am or for the positions I've taken over the years. I will absolutely explain and talk through my positions and how I came to them, but I won't pretend that I believe they were wrong. It nagged at me that their questions weren't really about substance. Rather, they were questioning my ideology, my approach, my world view. Again, it was their right to do so, but the manner in which they did suggested to me that they really didn't understand where the people who would decide this presidential election really were.

The questions kept coming: Did I think it would get awkward if my positions were at odds with the Vice President's? Are you going to have a hard time supporting her views? Will you have a hard time doing what she says? Don't you think your views would cause her to be embarrassed?

All I kept saying was this is what I believe, and these positions have been widely accepted here in Pennsylvania. I felt like my views could be an asset. I didn't see anything wrong with not aligning perfectly. The whole point isn't to agree on every single thing; you want to be able to hear each other out, listen, defend and challenge your own beliefs, and ultimately come to the strongest conclusion with a shared perspective.

Their job was to protect and serve the Vice President, and asking these questions was just carrying out that duty. In my mind, the best way to protect her would have been to figure out a way to expand her universe—both in terms of an actual base of support and in positions that weren't an exact issue-by-issue match but that would hopefully gel into a cohesive ideology and value system that voters could understand and rally behind. And they weren't going to expand her universe by doing the exact same thing that she had been doing all these years. With all due respect to Kamala's team, I was getting the feeling from the people around her on the vetting team that picking me as her running mate was something they thought they maybe *should* do, but they had reservations. And, for me, none of this was sitting right.

★   ★   ★

As the process with her campaign vetting team was winding down, Dana Remus asked me to meet over Zoom with a panel of more of Kamala's political and governmental advisers. Of course.

Remus ran it, and the panel included Nevada Senator Catherine Cortez Masto, former Labor Secretary Marty Walsh, former Associate Attorney General Tony West, who is also Kamala's brother-in-law, and former Congressman and White House adviser Cedric Richmond. They questioned me on a number of my positions, including a lot of the ones that went against the typical Democratic orthodoxy, like my stance on cutting taxes and energy policy.

The panel also spent a lot of time asking me about Israel. Why had I taken such a hard line on the protests happening on college campuses, particularly at the University of Pennsylvania? I had been critical of the protestors who were vandalizing the campus, assaulting and intimidating Jewish students, and shutting down the main quad. The people vetting me didn't seem to like what I had done. I told them that the safety of students on campus had been threatened, and I would take that position to protect them, or any other student group who's safety was at risk, any day. That many campuses had failed to maintain the balance between free speech and the safety of students on campus.

I wondered whether these questions were being posed to just me—the only Jewish guy in the running—or if everyone who had not held a federal office was being grilled about Israel in the same way.

What they did say was that they felt as though my positions were different from Kamala's views on the matter. I agreed that they were.

They were unsure of how our positions were going to blend. They asked me how I thought my views were going to play in Michigan, with such a large Arab American population.

Well, I said, I believed the same way it plays out in Pennsylvania. I have a very close relationship with our Muslim and Arab and Palestinian Christian communities here in Pennsylvania. I have for years. I go and meet with the communities. I respect them. I would do the same thing anywhere in this country. I'm not afraid to walk into any room. To listen. To handle criticism and tough questions from the people I seek to serve. I felt really good and clear about that.

I will just say: These sessions were completely professional and businesslike. But I just had a knot in my stomach through all of it. I was torn, caught between my head and my gut with the full recognition that it was a big deal to be vetted to be Vice President of the United States and, at the same time, that it just didn't feel like this was the right fit.

The other challenge was that there was really no one I could fully talk to about this, to gauge whether what I was feeling was a normal amount of doubt over an extremely consequential decision, or if this was particularly not right. The pool of people who had been in my shoes at that moment was so small. I couldn't comfortably ask Biden about it. I didn't really know Senator Tim Kaine. Obviously, Lori and I were discussing this every day and every night, but she was in Vancouver for the first part, and our vantage points were not exactly the same anyway.

With the VP vetting, only Lori and a small handful of my advisers and members of my team knew. At the same time, we were in a fishbowl, with the media looking in for clues, flying news helicopters over our home, standing outside of our house watching our kids play in the driveway, as if the answer to what was next would come from the swish of their jump shots—or mine (I'm still deadly from mid range even at 52). It was all at light speed, and there was no one around us who could really relate. The stakes were sky high. The higher they are, I learned unequivocally, the lonelier you can feel.

By Friday afternoon, Senator Catherine Cortez Masto called me. I had and still do have admiration for her leadership and career. She told me that she had been Attorney General, and while she had never been Governor, she understood what it was like to be an executive in an elected role, to actually be in charge. She had a good sense that I was an executive-minded person, as she put it, and that I needed to understand that I was only going to be number two as Vice President. That my job was to support the number one, to do what she says and to listen. I wouldn't be a decision maker.

Cortez Masto continued, but her point was made. Message received. I told her that I heard her, and that's part of what I was looking forward to speaking to Vice President Harris about. I got off the call with my gut and my head starting to align a bit more.

I would be meeting with Kamala over the weekend at the Vice President's Residence in Washington, but we were unclear about whether it would happen on Saturday or Sunday. For weeks, I had a bunch of events lined up for that weekend, and because of the scheduling uncertainty, we made the call to cancel them. Of course, that created its own media frenzy and speculation, which certainly added another element of pressure to the mix.

The small team of people I trusted to talk through all of this with sensed where I was heading and how bad it was starting to feel. Just pull out, they started suggesting. To them, if this was where my head was, there was no reason to even go ahead with the meeting. My response was that part of the reason I was feeling so uneasy because with all the vetting, with all the questioning, I hadn't yet spoken to Kamala about it. I had no sense of how she saw the role. How could I know if this would be the right fit if I didn't even have it properly defined?

Lori and I took a walk that evening to clear our heads before we sat down for Shabbat dinner with our family.

To Lori, none of this felt right. Particularly the weight of other people's expectations. She knew how they weighed on me. To both of us, it felt like people were deciding, thinking, feeling what they wanted for me, but their calculations didn't seem to factor in how this might impact our lives and our family, how their wishes might not be our own, how what was best for them might not be what was best for us. I knew that we could get excited about potentially jumping in and being part of something so important, but I had to be sure that we would be able to jump in with both feet, and we just didn't have that assurance at that moment.

Lori reminded me about the time when Senator Chuck Schumer was trying to convince me to run for Senate back in 2015 and how we made our decision not to run once we drowned out the noise and hype and focused on how best to serve and support our children at the same time.

As we walked our typical route that took us through the Penn State Abington campus, past the duck pond that I went to as a young boy with my grandparents, Lori looked at me.

"I think you are going to have regrets here no matter what happens," she said.

She knew that I would regret if I left my job as Governor that I was so enjoying, finding so much purpose in, for a job she thought I didn't really want to do. I'd have regrets if I moved my family to DC, away from their schools and their friends and family. And, likewise, I would regret pulling out before meeting with Kamala, and always wonder if I had not given the process a fair shake.

The decision, for both of us, had far greater ramifications beyond the personal. Lori knew the stakes of the election. I knew the stakes. I felt the weight of this through every step, in every breath. I believed I could help by being on the ticket. I felt confident in my standing in my home state of Pennsylvania, and I thought that could translate to giving us a better shot to beat Donald Trump in Pennsylvania and the other swing states. And, if that were the case, no matter what it meant for my family or me, no matter how wrong it might have felt internally, it was important to factor that into the decision making. It was about both what I wanted for my career and family and not at all about that. That very real pressure added to the gravity, and propelled me further into the process than maybe I would have gone if not for the consequence of it all.

I have never dwelled on regret in my life. Not because I haven't made mistakes or wished that in certain moments I would have made a different choice. But I am committed to learning from a mistake and keeping it moving. I knew that I would more regret not knowing. I was just agreeing to meet with her. Nothing more, nothing less. I also was very aware that it could very well not be offered to me. I knew it would be better to have all of the information on the table. That's how I always operated, so why should this moment be any different?

The hardest thing for Lori to stomach was her feeling like these expectations took something away from me. I loved my job. I was so happy doing it. I got to meet so many people, listen to what they need, and serve them.

Hesitant as she was, Lori told me that we would make it work for us, if offered, and if I decided that this was the right decision. We would figure it out.

My kids didn't love the process. They hated the media trucks outside. I know it annoyed them that their friends at camp that summer suddenly cared about what their dad was doing. They didn't like that we couldn't really walk our dog around the neighborhood with the feeding frenzy around us. They understandably didn't want their already different kind of childhood to be even more so. Jonah was a bit more open to it, perhaps because he had been there watching how it all played out from the beginning, so he felt a part of it. Sophia had a nuanced take. She had been working on the Biden campaign all summer, and, like most staffers, she was swiftly moved over to the Harris campaign as soon as he dropped out of the race. She understood the internal ropes better than any of us, and she was more skeptical of the idea than I had thought she might be.

But they all agreed that I should keep going until I was sure. Even with their own discomfort, they were a constant source of comfort and the softest place to land.

So I kept the meeting, which we found out late Friday night was set for Sunday.

I had already canceled my Saturday. Lori was taking the kids to meet up with friends in the Poconos, so I figured I might as well ride with them. I could go for a long walk and clear my head. At this point, I had stopped reading everything. I'd turned all the TVs off and tuned as much out as I possibly could. I always find that the less attention I pay to the noise, the better I am able to do my job and keep my head clear.

This was particularly true that week. There was a lot of praise about me as a potential pick, and there were also people out there trying to tear me down. I knew that there was also a ton of ugly antisemitic rhetoric and hate circulating online. "Genocide Josh," some called me online. I worried how this would impact my kids and just tried to keep them posted on the process every day and model how to manage all the noise. If I could ignore the hype, hopefully they could too. I tried to keep my head about me as much as I could, to keep my blinders on. I prayed a lot, about everything. I said the *Shema* more times during that week than maybe I had in my whole life before. I was asking for clarity. I needed it. I had faith that it would come.

We were in the Poconos with a bunch of other families to celebrate Jonah's girlfriend's mom's fiftieth birthday. Everyone there was wonderful, but also afraid to ask the obvious questions. I think some of them must have wondered why I was even there. Like most of our other friends and people we've grown up with along this journey, they were extremely encouraging. I knew that's how most people who knew me and supported me and voted for me felt. It comes from the most generous and loving place, and, man, did I appreciate all of the love and support I was feeling. There was a genuine belief that I could help avoid another four years of Trump, the degree to which that was true I really have no idea. Sometimes love and support, as well meaning as they are, can feel like a thing that you have to carry rather than a buoy that holds you up. That's what I was starting to feel. I headed home around dinnertime, knowing that I had an early morning the following day.

I slept fitfully, as I had every night throughout the vetting process. I tossed and turned until the sun came up, when I put on my suit and walked to the car in the driveway, where about a dozen reporters had been camped out for days. A few different trucks had tried to trail us, but we lost them pretty quickly. The vetting team had been worried that folks would follow us, so they had us switch cars when we got to DC and ride with a Harris aide and my security detail into the VP's Residence. I didn't quite understand the cloak-and-dagger routine, given that it had been widely reported that we were meeting that weekend, but it wasn't my process, and I was going along.

*   *   *

The ride to DC was mostly quiet apart from a call from Dana Remus. The vettors had just one more question before my meeting, she told me.

"Have you ever been an agent of the Israeli government?" she asked.

Had I been a double agent for Israel? Was she kidding? I told her how offensive the question was.

"Well, we have to ask," she said. "We just wanted to check." She added: "Have you ever communicated with an undercover agent of Israel?"

If they were undercover, I responded, how the hell would I know? I had been an Attorney General for my state. I understood what undercover work was and had dealt with and employed many undercover agents.

I calmly answered her questions. Remus was just doing her job. I get it. But the fact that she asked, or was told to ask that question by someone else, said a lot about some of the people around the VP.

*   *   *

I was five minutes early to our meeting at the Naval Observatory. On my way there, I was escorted by a member of the Naval Observatory team and made small talk. Later, I learned that small talk would be analyzed, misrepresented, and picked apart by members of the Vice President's team. Honestly, all I could think about was what this potential move might feel like for my kids. If they'd find a school they liked. Whether they could ever be comfortable in this as home.

The Vice President greeted me in the dining room, where they'd cleared out most of the furniture so the room had just a small table and two chairs at its center. There was a bench on the side, where two of her aides were sitting quietly to take notes during our meeting.

We got right to it. There was zero chitchat. Kamala told me how intense this was going to be because of what little time she had to mount this campaign. She expressed confidence that she had the momentum and would win the race. There were just three months until Election Day, and I would have to hit the ground running. I told her that I was extremely comfortable with that and used to that grind. I know how to stay on message and can work to the bone for a hundred days. That should be the least of her worries, I told her. She asked what I would need in terms of staff and logistics. I explained that I would need to have someone from the Governor's office with me, because I had to keep doing that job at the level I was used to while I was on the road. That was very important to me, to maintain that quality of work for Pennsylvania. She made the point that when she was on the campaign trail for Vice President, she separated herself from her work as senator, even though she represented one-eighth of the entire national population as senator of California. She expected my total focus. I told her that I would be fully committed, but being a senator is different from being a Governor. They require different things. I needed to maintain connectivity to my office in order to do my job, but that I knew it wouldn't be an issue to juggle both. I would be all in on the trail. Go everywhere they asked if they asked.

Could she win Pennsylvania without me? she asked. Maybe, I said. I really didn't know. It had only been a few weeks since she assumed the campaign from Biden. Polls were improving but Trump was still ahead in my home state. It was becoming more and more clear that I made the most sense for her politically, particularly with Pennsylvania as central to her victory as it was. Regardless, I would work every day until election day, no matter what role I had, to do all I could to make sure she got every last vote.

We quickly moved on to a few substantive issues, including Israel and the Middle East. She was focused on my stance. She asked if I would be willing to apologize for the statements I had made, particularly over what I saw happening at the University of Pennsylvania.

"No," I said flatly. I believe in free speech, and I'll defend it with all I've got. Most of the speech on campus, even that which I disagreed with, was peaceful and constitutionally protected. But some wasn't peaceful, was designed to instill fear and incite violence, and I wouldn't back down from calling that out.

I told her that's what I believed, and I have no problem going into a roomful of Muslim voters in Dearborn, Michigan, or in town halls with Palestinians or Christians or Arab Americans just about anywhere and listening to what they were feeling and what they believed. I have a strong relationship with those communities in Pennsylvania, and that wouldn't change if I campaigned nationally with her. She heard me and expressed how bad she felt that I had been getting hammered with the antisemitic attacks that she had witnessed throughout the process.

There wasn't much more issue-based conversation before we

moved on to what the vice presidency would look like in her administration. I told her that I knew I could serve her well on the campaign, which she seemed to accept, but that I wanted to hear more about how she envisioned the role if she won.

She explained that her time as Vice President had been tough. That she answered to President Biden's senior staff, and her schedule and priorities weren't her own. That a meeting she'd prepare for weeks for would get scrapped in an instant. But that was how it went. Your job was to serve the President, she said. That's it. I was surprised by how much she seemed to dislike the role. She noted that her chief of staff would be giving me my directions, lamented that the Vice President didn't have a private bathroom in their office, and how difficult it was for her at times not to have a voice in decision making.

"You need to remember that song '99 Problems,'" she said. "That's what it's like."

Your job, she explained to me is to make sure that you are not a problem for the President. That every day the President is trying to run the country and avoid World War III and your job is to do whatever is needed to support the President.

I pressed on.

I talked with her about how I approached my relationship with my governing partner, Lieutenant Governor Austin Davis. I had asked Austin, then a thirty-four-year-old state representative who would become our state's first Black Lieutenant Governor, to run on a ticket with me. He's an outstanding partner on the campaign trail and in governing. He is one of a small handful of people who can walk into my office at any point unannounced, and he always gets the chance to state his case, on anything, if he wants to. He's always heard. I wanted that same relationship with her. I told her that I knew I wasn't going to be the decision maker here. If we had door A and door B as options, and she was for door A and I was for door B, I just wanted to make sure that I could make the case for door B. And if I didn't convince her, then I'd run right through a brick wall to support her decision and make sure it succeeded. As long as I was heard.

She was crystal clear that that was not what she was looking for. I would primarily work with her staff. She couldn't say to me that I would have that kind of access to her.

To her great credit, she was completely honest with me. She was super direct and cordial, and that willingness to put her cards on the table and really lay out her expectations not only showed me great respect, but also allowed me to walk out of the room knowing full well everything I needed to know in order to understand the role.

We wrapped after about an hour. We shook hands, I thanked the aides who'd been silently taking notes, and as I started to leave, Vice President Harris stopped me. "I'd like you to stick around," she said. "I may want to talk to you later this evening." I told her that I needed to get back to Pennsylvania at some point that evening, but that I'd stay for a while.

Instead of going back the way we came in, my state police detail took an alternate route to former Attorney General Eric Holder's apartment, where the VP's team had asked me to wait. I assumed that she wanted me to meet with him, because he was running her vetting process with Remus. When I arrived, I was greeted by a young aide, who informed me that Holder was not there.

I entered Holder's apartment in downtown DC with a single member of my detail and was told to wait. I had no clue if there was anyone listening, or how long I'd be there. I went outside on a little balcony to call Lori to tell her about the meeting. I couldn't really talk, because I wasn't sure how private our conversation would actually be, so I mostly just sat there, in Holder's apartment, quietly. I was growing less and less patient and more and more sure that this was not what I wanted to sign up for. At one point, a tall young man came into the apartment. It turned out to be Eric's son, who lived there and, appropriately, seemed as surprised to see me as I was to see him. We had a nice exchange, and he left. I can't imagine what he was thinking.

After a couple of hours, I texted Remus and told her that I needed to head back home, but she asked me if I would be willing to stick around for a few minutes so that she could stop by and we could talk some more. When she got there, she sat me down at Eric's dining table and told me that she could sense that I didn't want to do this. It would be really hard for you, she said, with moving to DC. And it would be a real financial strain, she added. From the financial vetting, she said that she knew we didn't have a lot of money, and that Lori was going to have to get all new clothes and pay for people to do her hair and makeup, that we would have to pay for all of the food and entertainment at the Vice President's Residence, and that could be really challenging for us.

"Are you trying to convince me not to do this?" I asked, a little taken aback.

She explained that she just wanted to be sure that I wanted this before I talked to the Vice President again, so she was simply laying out the realities for me.

I told her that I wasn't going to go into a room with the Vice President again until I went home and talked this all through with my wife. I was a little slack-jawed. The comments were unkind to me. They were nasty to Lori. I hold no grudge against Remus, who I know was doing the job she had to do, but I needed to leave. I thanked her for her time and exited Holder's apartment.

When I got into the truck, I calmed down and prayed. I thought about those hours in that apartment and that final conversation. That is what my life would be if I took this job. It could have gone differently, had I left that meeting thinking that she would want a partner and someone to bounce things off of before she ultimately made her decision. There was a world in which it could have worked, but that was not this world. I was grateful for Kamala's candor, and the clarity it provided. I felt comfortable enough to be truthful right back.

Lori and the kids were waiting for me as I walked in the door. "What happened?" they asked us, eyes wide as baby deer, all of them. "Are you going to be the Vice President, Dad?" Reuben, our thirteen-year-old asked.

"I don't know, buddy," I said. "We are working through it. That's what we have to talk about."

"Dad," he said. "It doesn't seem like you want to do it." Then he walked away.

From the mouth of a teenage boy, no less.

In the middle of a period where every great mind was trying to articulate what was best for me and the party, what I wanted or didn't want, what Kamala wanted or didn't want, he just cut right on through it. As sweet and innocent as it was precise, like a knife.

It is an amazing thing as a parent, when you watch your kid transition from this little being to a sharp observer of the world. The moment where you see your kid seeing things. And in this moment, my son was seeing me, in the midst of a period when others were projecting what they wanted for me, what they thought I might want or would be useful to them for me to want.

These were my people. This was my path. I didn't need to hear anything else.

*   *   *

After dinner, Lori and I sat at the edge of our bed, hashing it out. I recounted all the points of my meeting earlier that day. On one hand, I was still tugged by the prestige of it all. It's an honor. It's a big title. But that's never been enough for me. It never would or could be. And on the other hand, I felt the nagging pull of what it would mean if I withdrew from the running because the stakes of this election were so high and we all had a responsibility to do our part. There were so many people—those I know and love and care about, and many more I've never met but whose hopes I felt keenly—who so wanted this for me. The weight of those expectations was hard to shake. But it wasn't my race to lose or win. People were going to cast their votes for her, or they weren't.

"All right," I said to Lori. "I'm not doing this. I'm not going to do it. I don't want to do this."

I didn't know what was going to happen next, but I knew that we would be in the driver's seat, on our own road. Wherever we decide to take it, we decide where it goes, and when to get on or off.

It has been true my entire career that in the run-up to these big life decisions, I need to work to find my center. But the moment I come to a decision, I never look back. Ever. Lori reiterated her concerns about regrets. I had none. I was at peace. I wasn't going to look back and say, did I make the wrong choice? I was going to continue serving the people who had elected me in Pennsylvania, to stay in a role that served them, a role that I loved. I was doing what was right for my family, certainly. That was without question. And I knew then that this was unquestionably right for me, too.

I had prayed for clarity.

And now I was nothing but clear.

*   *   *

I called Dana, my Chief of Staff, to tell her what I decided. Saul pressed me to put out a statement that night, saying that I had withdrawn myself from consideration. Our team was really split on it, and I understood both sides of the argument. It was ultimately my choice and we deserved to be able to tell that truth on our own terms, but I pushed back and came to the conclusion that it wouldn't be fair to Kamala if we put out our own statement. This was her process.

After we batted it around internally, I thought I owed it to Remus to give her a call and let her know that I had reflected on our conversation and I didn't want to go forward in the process.

I called her, told her where I had landed, and asked to talk directly with the VP to inform her. It was around eight-thirty at night, but Remus said she had retired for the evening and wouldn't be available to speak to me. I pressed her. She then told me that the VP would not handle bad news well and that I shouldn't push. At that point, I left it to the VP's team to let her know about what I had decided.

I got into bed feeling nothing but relief. For the first time in two weeks, I slept.

I drove to Harrisburg that Monday morning to break the news to my senior team in person, to explain my decision and how I got there. I was dreading this part, honestly. I figured that they would be disappointed, that the path to DC they'd perhaps started daydreaming about was ending there, because I had decided that I wanted out. I told them that I withdrew in large measure because I love what I was doing there, in that building, with them. I choked up. Some of them did, too. I thought it was because they were disappointed, which of course weighed heavily on me. I rely on these people every day. I love them and care for them and respect them. Before then, I hadn't been able to talk to them about any of this, which felt secretive and hard and not true to myself or our bond.

Cleansing as it was not to have to hold back the truth anymore, I now faced the real prospect that I'd be letting down the people I cared so much about. I later learned that I could not have been more wrong.

"Are you insane?" Dana, my Chief of Staff, said. "No one wanted you to do this. We are all thrilled." Let's just get back to work, I said.

* * *

That Monday, the Harris camp still hadn't announced a pick. We knew that I was out, but the world did not, which felt surreal. On one hand, I felt a million pounds lighter having found my inner clarity. On the other hand, there were people still expecting me to be the pick. The media was still all around: my basketball game to blow off steam with Max in the driveway of our family home made its way onto the cable channels that night, thanks to the bank of cameras still parked outside our home. I hit my midrange jumpers against Max, but he beat me in our pickup game. We had dinner all together that night, relaxed and laughing and connected in a way none of us had felt in weeks.

We woke up the next morning to helicopters flying overhead

and the boys headed off to camp as usual, which confused some people. How were we sending them off to camp at a time like this? We already knew the thing that the others were waiting to find out. The great mystery had been solved for us by then, but for everyone else, the announcement wasn't coming until later in the morning.

Kamala called me to tell me she officially had chosen Tim Walz, a friend of mine and a good man for whom I have real respect and affection. She could not have been nicer. I still had no idea whether Dana Remus and the rest of her team had shared that I'd called to inform them I didn't want to move forward the night after our meeting. I told her how excited I was by her choice. I meant it. We both reiterated that this was the right way for us to work together, and that I would hustle for her on the trail over the next three months how ever she needed me.

Once news broke that Walz was the pick, the stream of "I'm sorry" texts rushed in. So many people reached out expressing just how disappointed and let down they were that it wasn't me.

I felt better than I had in weeks. I knew how this played out. This was what I wanted, but they didn't know that. I could feel how long of a day this was about to be already.

We crafted a statement. I explained that I had gone through the vetting process and met with Kamala directly about her vision for the role and the future. "As I've said repeatedly over the past several weeks, the running mate decision was a deeply personal decision for the Vice President—and it was also a deeply personal decision for me. Pennsylvanians elected me to a four-year term as their Governor, and my work here is far from finished—there is a lot more stuff I want to get done for the good people of this Commonwealth." I added that she had my enthusiastic support, as did Tim, and that I'd be out there traveling all across the Commonwealth to unite Pennsylvanians behind their campaign.

Their first joint event together was that evening, in of all places, Philadelphia. To be honest, I didn't really want to go. I was wrung out. I just wanted to be home with my family, to take a walk with Lori, and just be. But this was my city, my Commonwealth, and I knew that I wanted to show my very real support for the ticket.

Lori and I were happy to see Tim and Gwen Walz—whom we both were so happy for—in the basement of the Liacourus Center in North Philly and offer them our support for the road ahead. We spent time with Kamala and her husband, Doug Emhoff, who's been a friend for many years. Sophia, who was working the event in her official capacity as a staffer, came by, too. We hugged and took photos, and within a few minutes, I was being ushered toward the hold backstage and told that I was up next to go out there and speak. I had no prepared remarks and was given a simple task of expressing my support for the new ticket. There were fifteen thousand people in that arena. The rush of those last two weeks had been so intense and taxing that I hadn't even thought about the fact that I had to go out there and address that crowd, at a moment when I knew every one of those people had feelings about the stakes of the election, about Kamala, about her pick for Vice President. I looked to Lori, who was walking along beside me in the bowels of the arena.

"What am I supposed to say?" I asked.

"I have absolutely no idea," she responded. "You'll think of something." Quite the pep talk.

I took my time getting to the podium as I walked the long catwalk toward the stage, both to buy a little more time to come up with what I would say and to soak in the magnitude of that moment. I took note of the familiar faces in the hall. The people who had been there for me in my past campaigns. The people who had my back. The people who knew me best. I was overcome with emotion.

I looked around that room and just spoke from my heart, about how much I loved being their Governor and that I wasn't going anywhere. How I take pride in my faith and the important work ahead to elect Kamala and Tim. How I was all in for them. For the time I was on that stage, I felt the warmth and the love in that room; I wished I could have bottled it.

Lori and Sophia were waiting for me as I stepped offstage, both of them with tears in their eyes. I can't think of a single other time that I did anything remotely impressive enough to move Lori to tears. Lori looked at me and said, "That may have been the best speech you have ever given."

I knew the choice I had made was not easy to get to. It was certainly not the conventional one. It required a great deal of letting go—of expectation, of outside noise. But there was no doubt in my mind, as I saw their faces. That I'd done good. I knew I would campaign hard for the ticket in the coming months, and I did—traveling across Pennsylvania and the country, filming a TV ad with Kamala, and leaving it all on the field for our ticket.

I prayed for clarity, and found it.

CHAPTER VII

Light Keepers

FIVE MONTHS LATER, IN THE weeks following the arson attack on the Residence, as I sat in a pew at Salem Baptist Church, I felt a tap on my arm. It was a woman from the congregation who had been sitting in the pew across from me. She was in a baby-pink T-shirt and sweatpants and a matching baseball cap, suited up to join the other church ladies on a fitness walk after the service. She was in her seventies, at least, and greeted me with a smile. "Governor, I've been praying for you," she said. I was touched, of course. "We will take care of you like you took care of me all those years ago and lifted me up."

She had tears in her eyes as she told me that seventeen years ago, when I'd served this district in the state House, we had met at a local event. Her husband had been sick, and she'd been having a hard time. They'd needed help with their medical benefits. I'd heard her, she said. I could see how down and out they had been. I'd told my team that they needed to figure out a way to get them what they needed, and we had. And now, here she was, in this church, at a difficult point in my life and for my family. She was here praying for me, lifting me up. I could feel the power of her prayers. The sense of connectedness to someone I hadn't really seen in many years.

Those days after the attack on the Governor's Residence felt, at times, heavy and unrelenting, like we were wandering through the dark. And yet, as we navigated the challenges and shouldered the weight, what we remember most is not the hardness and the weight. What we carry forward are the moments like this. Because this light, it was all around us. We were overwhelmed by the outpouring from people all across this country whose shared humanity, shared sense of decency, shared agreement of what is right and what is wrong and of what our country should be and who Americans are at our core, overrides all of that.

In days like that morning at Salem, or when I am in a synagogue or any place of worship, which is often in the course of my work, I find myself thinking more and more about William Penn. That he arrived on our shores in October 1682 aboard a ship named *Welcome.* His Pennsylvania would be a place that would be open to all people, grounded in free expression, freedom of religion, free elections, and respect for others. I think about my responsibility to carry this forward—to go a few more miles in the journey Penn began, to build a place that remains warm and welcoming for everyone—no matter what you look like, where you come from, who you love, or who you pray to.

Now, I assume Penn could have never imagined a Governor who prays like me or a Lieutenant Governor who looks like Austin in the land he once led. Or that he ever would have envisioned a world in which a Jewish Governor would host a giant iftar during Ramadan, obsess about needing more and bigger Christmas trees at the Governor's Residence in December, or host his son's bar mitzvah in the same spot where both of those expressions of other people's faiths took place. Though I do bet he'd be proud of how far we've come.

His ideas of faith and his acceptance of others set in motion something that we need to find our way back to today. It's a foundational principle of this great nation. A band of patriots gathered at Independence Hall in 1776 to declare our independence from a king and set ourselves on a path of self-determination. Those patriots plotted, planned, and organized in taverns and town squares and decided that they wanted to live in a place grounded in the notion of real freedom and self-determination. And over the last two and half centuries, our American story has been defined by people from all walks of life who have followed that lead and done their part. Ordinary Americans rising up, demanding more, seeking justice, and working to build a better life for their children. The story of our nation has not been written just by people with titles next to their names or by people in government offices but by everyday folks believing in each other, standing up, raising their voices, and using their power.

I've been privileged in my life to know those people—the ones who will be in the history books and the ones I've written about in this book. The ones I feel blessed to know because they taught me something and helped me grow as a public servant, as a father, a husband, and a person, and brought me closer to my own faith.

That is the American way. Those are the bonds that lead to a more perfect union. Those people, those bonds, that deeper connection to my faith are how I have learned to fish differently. To show up, to listen, to leave this place better than we found it. That's the cornerstone of my faith—of all faiths, really. It's elemental, even as it is sometimes hard to see and feel today.

This has been true at all the most significant moments in American history—the commitment to doing the hard work required to have faith in these ideals and the people to perfect them. That is our shared story. It was true for our Founders at Independence Hall. It offered courage to the brave souls who wore our uniform and landed on foreign beaches to protect our freedoms here at home and defeat fascism abroad. It was on display when our neighbors, who sought a more perfect union, sat down at the lunch counter so the next generation could stand taller.

I've witnessed this in the many millions of quieter moments of goodness, too. The way my father showed faith that new moms could tell him what they needed for their babies, not the other way around. The way my mother taught me to care about the world around me. In how the survivors of abuse found the courage to expose the truth. I've seen this with the dedication and bravery of the Hawbaker workers who were unafraid of corporate power. And with the law enforcement officers who care so deeply about their neighbors that they're willing to give their lives for the rest of us. I witnessed the fortitude of moms who lost their kids to fentanyl, who turn their pain into help for others; the craftsmen who wouldn't let an arsonist's crimes keep the people's home closed; the brave couples who pushed for marriage equality and moved the needle; the lady at Sheetz who got her husband the care he needed, along with thousands of others in dire straits; a community ravaged by an attack on their neighbors determined to show a capacity to love rather than succumb to hate.

All those people and their actions and their belief in common good have propelled us forward, just like our Founders intended, and helped us find our faith in a brighter, better day. Ordinary folks doing extraordinary things each day to build a more just and connected nation. To not be consumed by darkness or chaos.

Now more than ever, we yearn for and need a world defined

by faith. It's universal, this belief in others to help us through what feels unsettled, uncivil, un-American. It's a guidepost, a path through the woods. When the dark feels like it could consume us whole and churn us up and lose us, it is where we keep the light.

ACKNOWLEDGMENTS

Notwithstanding being cut from the basketball team in college, hoops remains an important part of my life. I love to play, coach my kids, watch on the couch with the family, text with my buddies during the game, call into sports radio and analyze the game from the night before. I can't hoop like I used to but the lessons I took with me from the game are central in my work today.

Basketball is a team sport. That team mentality is infused in everything I do—personally and professionally.

I am grateful to the team that helped me create *Where We Keep the Light*. Jay Mandel and Gail Ross of WME who had my back and supported me along the way. Sean Desmond and the team at Harper who believed in me and how my story could appeal to our better angels.

And, of course, Emily Jane Fox, whose writing skills are exemplary and who has a unique ability to pull strings and then tie them all together. Thank you for turning my love for my family, faith, and service into a book that I hope my children will read one day.

Throughout my career, I've had the good fortune to work with exceptionally talented and dedicated professionals who are deeply committed to public service. I've been especially blessed to work in Pennsylvania with Team GSD, led by Dana Fritz, who believe in me and in each other and our ability to leave things a little better than we found them. Dana has been my right hand for more than a decade. Her know-how, mind-melding abilities, work ethic, and unique feel for the game allows us to put points on the board every day for our fellow Pennsylvanians.

Mom, Dad, Ellie, John, and Saul who always show up for us, and love us unconditionally. L'dor v'dor.

To Rebecca, Adam, Jon, Rena, and my incredible nieces and nephews, thank you for your love, your support, and for making sure the next generation remains a strong, united team.

Sophia, Jonah, Max, and Reuben, you are my everything—my reason for doing what I do. I know you've made so many personal sacrifices so that I can serve, and at the same time, I hope you've been able to see up close the real meaning of tikkun olam.

To the captain of the team in every way, the love of my life since the ninth grade, Lori. You bring the light and the love, and together we've built a wonderful life of purpose and principle. This book, and the stories in them, do not exist but for you. With all my heart and all my soul, I love you always.

ABOUT THE AUTHOR

JOSH SHAPIRO is the 48th Governor of Pennsylvania. He previously served as Pennsylvania's Attorney General, Chair of the Montgomery County Board of Commissioners, and State Representative of Pennsylvania. From seeing his parents serve others—his father in the Navy and as the local pediatrician and his mother as an educator—to marrying his high school sweetheart, Lori, and raising four children in the community and traditions they grew up in, to a career fighting for the people of Pennsylvania, Governor Shapiro's life has been grounded in faith, family, and public service.